THE ROWLEY COOKBOOK

DEPRESSION-ERA COOKING FOR BODY, SOUL AND CHERISHED FRIENDSHIPS

Compiled by Amy Goebel Padgett

The Rowley Cookbook

COPYRIGHT © 2009 by Amy Goebel Padgett

Contact information: amy@amypadgett.com

Cover Art by Amy Goebel Padgett

Publishing History
First Edition, 2009

DEDICATION

This book is gratefully dedicated to all the cooks, friends and family who have shared their recipes. Below are a few contributors to this cookbook. If I forgot anyone or misspelled a name, please forgive me.

Grandma and Grandpa: Mary Irene and Gordon Rowley

Mrs. Akerhaugen, Berline Baldwin,
Mrs. Bowles, Mrs. Bronson,
Mrs. MacDonald, Esther Hathaway,
Alice & Effie Farrell, Mrs. Fletcher,
Mary "Betty" and Laurence G. Goebel,
Mrs. Graham, Inez Hathaway,
Virginia Herrick, Hilda Hephew,
Mrs. Kammer, Mrs. Kruse,
Bernice Lee, Mary and Helen Manney,
Minnie Mae Phillips Rowley, Mrs. Nelson,
Mrs. Irene Padgett, George and Dorothy Pfielsticker,
Dot Russell, Mrs. Olin,
Vera Olson, Mrs. Rule,
Marge Schroeder, Adah Shimer,
Don Vader, Myrtle Vader,
Mrs. Henry Verhagen, and Mrs. Rose Verhagen

FOREWORD

This cookbook is truly a labor of love. After scanning the pages of our family's tattered cookbook, handed down for three generations, I wanted to duplicate it for all of my cousins, relatives, and friends who had cherished memories of my grandmother's wonderful cooking. Publishing the recipes seemed like the perfect solution.

One glance at the table of contents will tell you that my grandmother always had a house full of friends and neighbors who came over for a chat, a cup of coffee and something sweet to eat every night. There are a lot of recipes for cakes, pies and cookies, and they all speak of the love and friendship shared.

My grandmother and grandfather created the original cookbook out of a ledger book soon after their marriage. Together, they entered recipes from 1917 through 1960 when my grandfather passed away.

I've taken the liberty of adding a few recipes handed down to my husband from his mother before she passed away, as well, and recipes from friends. I know my grandmother would approve. My mother-in-law was a wonderful German lady who, like my grandmother, loved to share food with friends and especially liked a cup of coffee and a lovely strudel or cake in the afternoon.

The recipes are good, solid home cooking, intended to stretch the budget and provide food for both the body and spirit. Grandmother was a wonderful baker and always made a magical, delicious treat each day to entertain friends and family who dropped in after dinner. There are many recipes collected from, and useful for, church socials, club meetings, picnics, and other special events.

Many recipes may be familiar to folks under other titles. But my grandparents frequently added or entitled collected recipes with the name of the friend or family member who contributed it. I kept this precedence and did not try to find the "correct title" for the recipe. I also kept the names of contributors, as indicated in the original cookbook. It is an informal but grateful tribute to all the cooks who made the collection possible.

And in addition to the fabulous desserts, there are a lot of hot dishes, or what others call casseroles. There is nothing like a hot dish to stretch the budget, so these recipes were very prevalent during the depression.

I still love these delicious hot dishes. Whenever I'm sad or feeling nostalgic, I crave their easy, warm comfort, with my particular favorite being the Nelson Hot Dish. Nothing tastes better than a steaming plate filled with a casserole in the dead of winter after a long walk in the snow.

After my grandfather passed away in 1960, my grandmother moved in with us and split her time between our home and our cousins' home in California. During this period, when my sister and I got home from school, there would always be fresh bread or rolls, and something special for after dinner. If she baked a pie, she took the pie crust trimmings, sprinkled them with cinnamon and sugar, rolled them into "snails" the size of a nickel that she baked in a small copper pan. So on pie days, we could have our cinnamon snails as a snack, too, to tide us over until dinner.

Please note: some of the recipes were merely lists of ingredients with no directions at all. I've tried to supply at least rudimentary instructions. For grandmother, these lists were intended more as reminders so she wouldn't forget a critical ingredient. She knew how to cook—all she needed was the list of ingredients.

To provide additional help, I've included some basic material in the appendix. It consists of simple weights/measures, substitutions, and that sort of thing.

If the order of recipes seems a little arbitrary, it's because I tried to stay true to the original cookbook as much as possible.

For the very young among you: an "ice box" is a refrigerator.

I hope you enjoy the collection!

TABLE OF CONTENTS

BREADS, MUFFINS & WAFFLES

CRANBERRY BREAD

    2 c. flour
    1 c. sugar
    1½ tsp. baking powder
    ½ tsp. baking soda
    1 tsp. salt
    ¼ c. shortening
    ¾ c. orange juice
    1 Tbsp. grated orange rind
    1 egg
    ½ c. chopped nuts
    1 c. cranberries, coarsely chopped

Sift flour, sugar, baking powder, salt, and baking soda together. Cut in shortening until mixture resembles coarse cornmeal. Beat egg. Add orange juice and rind to egg. Pour all at once into dry ingredients. Mix just enough to dampen dough. Carefully fold in nuts and cranberries. Spoon into a greased loaf pan, 9x5x3" and bake in a 350° oven until toothpick comes out clean.

SUGAR-COATED MUFFINS

        2 c. flour
        2 Tbsp. sugar
        2-½ tsp. baking powder
        (Sift the 3 preceding ingredients together)
        3/4 tsp. salt
        1 egg
        3/4 c. milk
        1/3 c. shortening

Mix together and bake at 350° for approximately 20 minutes.

        1 c. sugar
        1 tsp. cinnamon
        ½ c. butter

Mix sugar and cinnamon in a sack or plastic bag. Melt butter and drop muffins in melted butter and then shake in the sack of sugar & cinnamon.

KOLACKY

        1 cake yeast
        2 Tbsp. milk
        ½ tsp. salt
        1 lemon rind, grated
        ½ c. shortening
        4 egg yolks
        3 c. flour
        4 Tbsp. sugar
        1 c. hot sweet cream (thin)

Dissolve yeast in 2 Tbsp. warm milk with ½ tsp. sugar. Mix flour and shortening with salt as for pie dough. Beat egg yolks and add cream, sugar, & lemon rind, and add flour/butter mixture softened with raised yeast. Set aside in cool place overnight. Roll out when ready to bake to about ¼" thick. Cut with cookie cutter. Fill with cooked dried prunes or apricots (see below).

Let raise double in bulk. Bake in 350° oven for 20-25 minutes.

Cook prunes with little water, remove pits, cut fine. Use 1 tsp. in center, pinch dough together.

GRAHAM BREAD

    1 c. brown sugar
    2 ½ c. sour milk
    2 eggs
    2 c. graham flour
    2 c. white flour
    2 tsp. baking soda
    2 tsp. baking powder
    1 c. raisins
    1 tsp. salt
    2 Tbsp. shortening

Can use ½ c. raisins, ½ c. nut meats instead of 1 c. raisins. Bake in 2 loaf pans for 1 hour in a moderate (350°) oven.

BRAN BREAD

    2 eggs
    1 ½ c. brown sugar
    2 c. sour milk
    2 c. flour
    1 tsp. baking soda
    2 c. bran flakes
    1 tsp. salt
    nuts & raisins (as desired)

Bake 1 hour in a moderate (350°) oven.

BLUEBERRY MUFFINS

½ c. butter, creamed

¼ c. sugar

1 egg beaten lightly

¼ tsp. salt

2 c. sifted flour

Pinch of salt

4 tsp. baking powder

1 c. milk

1 c. blueberries (mix some of flour with berries)

Cream butter. Add sugar, salt, egg, alternately with milk & flour sifted with baking powder. Then fold in berries. Bake in well-greased muffin pan about 25 minutes.

CORN BREAD

1 Tbsp. butter

2 eggs

1 c. milk

1 c. cornmeal

1 Tbsp. lard

3/4 c. sugar

1 c. flour

2 tsp. baking powder

Bake in shallow pan for about 25 minutes at 400°.

WAFFLES

  3 c. buttermilk

  1 tsp. baking soda

  2 eggs

  1 Tbsp. sugar

  1 tsp. baking powder

  4 Tbsp. melted butter

  Pinch of salt

  2 c. flour to begin with, use more if needed

Beat eggs. Add wet ingredients, then add dry. Pour into heated and greased waffle iron.

DOUGHNUTS

  3 eggs

  1 c. sugar

  4 Tbsp. melted butter

  1 c. sour milk

  1 tsp. baking soda

  Flour

  1 tsp. cream of tartar

  Pinch of Salt

  1 tsp. Vanilla

  Pinch of Nutmeg

Mix wet ingredients, then add dry. Add only enough flour to create workable dough. Cut out with a doughnut cutter and fry in hot oil.

CINNAMON-TOPPED BREAD

    2 c. flour
    4 tsp. baking powder
    ¼ tsp. salt
    3 Tbsp. sugar
    5 Tbsp. shortening
    1 egg
    1 c. milk
    ½ c. brown sugar
    1 tsp. cinnamon

Mix together flour, baking powder, salt & sugar. Cut in the fat, add egg and milk. Pour into a shallow, square pan. Sprinkle with brown sugar and cinnamon. Bake 20 minutes in a moderate (350°) oven. Cut in bars.

LAURA'S COFFEE CAKE

    ½ c. sugar
    ¼ tsp. salt
    ½ tsp. cinnamon
    3 level tsp. baking powder
    1 c. flour
    ½ c. milk
    1 egg beaten
    4 Tbsp. melted butter.

Sift dry ingredients together. Add milk, egg and butter. Bake in greased pan. Slice apples on top if desired. Sprinkle with cinnamon and sugar. Bake 10 minutes in hot (450°) oven.

MUFFINS

2 c. flour
1 Tbsp. sugar
3 level Tbsp. lard or shortening
4 level tsp. baking powder
1 c. water or milk

Mix all ingredients lightly. Bake 15 minutes in muffin tins.

GINGER BREAD

½ c. shortening
½ c. sugar
1 c. molasses
Cream preceding 3 together
2 eggs
2 c. sifted flour
1 tsp. baking soda
1 tsp. ginger
1 tsp. salt
½ tsp. cinnamon

Add dry ingredients alternately with ½ c. milk; add to first mixture, beat well. Bake at 350 degrees for 45 minutes.

QUICK ROLLS (DOT RUSSELL)

1 cake yeast
2-½ c. warm milk

Cream in mixing bowl: ½ c. shortening, 2 Tbsp. sugar, 2 tsp. salt

Stir in 5 c. flour. Let rise in pan till double in bulk (about 2 hours). Punch down, drop in greased muffin tins. Let rise. Bake in quick oven (450°) about 15 minutes.

MARGIE'S BREAD

    2 yeast cakes
    1 c. lukewarm water
    2 Tbsp. brown sugar

Combine these 3 and let set while mixing other ingredients.

    6 c. brown flour (don't sift)
    4 c. unsifted white flour
    ½ c. brown sugar
    1/3 c. oil
    3/4 c. powdered milk
    3 c. lukewarm water
    2 tsp. salt

Mix these ingredients, and use oil on hands to knead. Let stand 5 minutes. Shape into loaves and let rise until double and bake at 325° for about 1 hour to 1 hour 20 minutes. Bread will be sticky but wheat flour will absorb it. Grease pans well. Makes three loaves.

FRUIT WAFFLES

    2 c. flour
    4 tsp. baking powder
    1/8 tsp. salt
    1 Tbsp. sugar
    2 eggs
    1 ½ c. water
    3 Tbsp. melted butter
    ½ c. crushed fruit

Beat 2 egg yolks until light. Add water. Sift flour, baking powder, sugar and salt together. Stir into mixture. Add fruit, butter and fold in egg whites. Cook in a greased and heated waffle iron.

DATE NUT BREAD

 1 c. chopped dates
 2 Tbsp. butter
 1 ½ tsp. baking soda
 ¼ tsp. salt
 1 c. boiling water
 1 tsp. vanilla
 ½ c. chopped nut meats
 1 ½ c. flour
 2 eggs

Mix dates, butter, soda, salt and water. Add other ingredients, pour into well greased loaf pan. Let stand 10 minutes, then bake 40 minutes in a slow oven - 350 or 325°.

REFRIGERATOR ROLLS (ADAH SHIMER)

 2 c. boiling water
 ½ c. sugar
 1 Tbsp. salt
 8 c. sifted flour
 2 unbeaten eggs
 2 Tbsp. shortening
 2 cakes compressed yeast
 ¼ c. lukewarm water

Mix boiling water, ½ c. sugar & shortening together. Cool until lukewarm, soak yeast in 1/4 lukewarm water. Add 1 tsp. sugar. Stir into first mixture. Add unbeaten eggs, stir in 4 c. flour, beat thoroughly. Knead in rest of flour. Brush top with shortening. Put in cool place to rise. Put in tins 2 hours before baking in 375° oven.

COMFITS (MRS. VERHAGEN)

　　1 c. sugar
　　2 beaten eggs
　　2 c. milk, beat well

Add 3 good c. flour sifted with 2 tsp. baking powder, 1 tsp. salt to milk mixture. Add 1 tsp. vanilla. Let rise for 30 minutes. Have about 2 lbs lard hot. Drop dough by tsp. in hot fat. Brown well. When cool, sugar.

BANANA BREAD

　　½ c. shortening
　　1 c. sugar
　　2 eggs
　　3 Tbsp. sour milk
　　2 mashed bananas
　　2 c. flour
　　1 tsp. baking soda
　　¼ tsp. salt

Cream butter & sugar, add eggs and mix. Add bananas, milk with soda, salt and flour. Bake in 350° oven for 45 minutes (in a loaf pan).

ENGLISH MUFFINS

　　1 cake yeast
　　1 c. scalded milk, cooled
　　1 c. lukewarm water
　　2 Tbsp. sugar
　　4 Tbsp. lard or shortening
　　6 c. sifted flour
　　1 tsp. salt

Dissolve yeast and sugar in lukewarm liquid, add shortening and 3 c. of flour. Beat until smooth, add rest of flour and salt. Place in roll, grease top. Let rise in warm place until double in bulk, about 2 hours. Makes 12 muffins.

APPLESAUCE NUT BREAD

> 2 c. flour
> 3/4 c. sugar
> 3 tsp. baking powder
> 1 tsp. salt
> 2 Tbsp. melted butter
> ½ tsp. cinnamon
> 1 c. nut meats
> 1 egg
> 1 c. apple sauce
> 1 tsp. baking soda

Sift dry ingredients. Add nuts, mix eggs, applesauce and melted shortening. Add dry ingredients and stir only to blend. Pour into loaf pans. Bake at 350° for 1 hour.

NUT BREAD

> 2 well beaten eggs
> 2 c. brown sugar
> 2 c. sour milk
> 1 tsp. baking powder
> 2 tsp. baking soda
> 2 c. nut meats
> 4 c. flour

Beat eggs and sugar thoroughly, add milk and beat well. Add sifted dry ingredients and nuts. Bake in greased loaf pan at 350° for 1 hour.

BANANA APPLE CRISP

4 apples
3 bananas
½ c. flour
Juice of 1 lemon
¼ c. water
4 Tbsp. butter
3/4 c. brown sugar

Arrange layer of fruit in baking dish. Sprinkle with flour/sugar mixture. cover with lemon juice and water. Dot with butter. Bake 1 hour at 350°.

CHILDREN'S BUNS

1 cake yeast
2 c. milk, scalded and cooled
1 Tbsp. sugar
6 c. sifted flour
½ c. butter
1 c. sugar
1 egg
1 c. currants
½ tsp. salt

Dissolve yeast and 1 Tbsp. sugar in lukewarm milk. Add three c. flour to make sponge. Beat well. Cover and set in warm place to rise about one hour. When light, add butter and sugar creamed, egg well beaten, currants, which have been floured*, rest of flour and salt. Knead lightly and let rise in greased bowl in warm place about 2 or 2 ½ hours. Put it in well greased pans, let rise about 1 hour or until double in size. Brush with egg diluted with milk. Bake 15 minutes or 20 in hot (450°) oven (425°). Can be sprinkled with powdered sugar.

QUICK ORANGE ROLLS

2 c. sifted flour
4 tsp. baking powder
1 tsp. salt
4 Tbsp. shortening
3/4 to 1 c. milk
Orange juice
Sugar lumps (sugar squares)

Sift dry ingredients, add shortening, add milk and mix quickly. Drop into greased muffin tins. On top of each roll place a sugar lump dipped in orange juice.

NUT BREAD (DATES OR RAISINS)

1 egg
1 c. brown sugar
1 c. sour milk
1 tsp. baking soda
3 Tbsp. shortening
Pinch of salt
½ c. nut meats
2 c. flour
1 c. dates or raisins, cut fine

Bake in loaf tin at 350 to 375° for 1 hour or until done.

APPLESAUCE BREAD

    3/4 c. sugar
    3 tsp. Baking powder
    1 Tbsp. melted butter
    ½ tsp. cinnamon
    1 c. apple sauce
    1 tsp. baking soda in a little water
    1 c. nut meats
    1 egg

Sift dry ingredients. Add nuts. Mix eggs, apple sauce, shortening. Stir only to blend. Put in loaf pan and bake for 1 hour at 350°.

JOHNNY CAKE

    3/4 c. corn meal
    1 c. flour
    ¼ c. sugar
    4 tsp. baking powder
    ½ tsp. salt
    1 beaten egg
    1 c. milk
    2 Tbsp. fat, melted

Sift dry ingredients together. Add well beaten egg, milk and melted fat. Beat well. Bake 20 minutes in hot (450°) oven.

(Can use 1 c. sour milk, ½ tsp. baking soda and 2 tsp. baking powder instead.)

JULE KAGA

3 Quarts milk (canned may be used, dilute though)

2 c. sugar

1 large yeast cake, add to lukewarm milk

3/4 c. shortening

2 tsp. cardamom

1 tsp. salt

Mix dough like for bread. Let rise, punch down, let rise again, then add ¼ lb of white raisins, 2 oz of citron to each loaf. Work into dough until evenly mixed. Bake in moderate oven, 350°.

DUMPLINGS

2 c. flour

3 tsp. baking powder

1 egg

¼ tsp. salt

Milk to make a stiff dough. Drop into boiling stew. Cook for 20 minutes more.

POTATO PANCAKES (LARRY GOEBEL)

2 or 3 potatoes, peeled

1 onion

1 egg, beaten slightly

Flour, salt and pepper

Grind the potatoes and onion together, keeping the liquid with the pulp. Mix in the egg, a tsp. of salt and ½ tsp. of pepper, then begin adding flour by the Tbsp. until the mixture assumes the consistency of pancake batter.

Heat a griddle and fry as you would any other pancake. Best fried in bacon grease if you have any.

This recipe can be increased or decreased as desired. You can also substitute squash for the potatoes.

CAKES

SPONGE CAKE

    1 ½ c. cake flour
    1¼ tsp. baking powder
    ½ tsp. salt
    4 eggs
    1¼ c. sugar
    1 tsp. vanilla
    1 tsp. grated lemon rind
    2/3 c. boiling water

Sift flour, baking powder and salt together. Beat the egg yolks gradually until thick and light. Add ½ c. of sugar, gradually beating constantly.

Beat egg whites until thick and foamy. Add remaining 3/4 c. of sugar gradually and continue beating until stiff enough to hold peaks. Add vanilla and lemon rind.

Add boiling water to egg yolks, stirring well. Add flour at once, beat with spoon until smooth. Fold into egg whites. Turn into 9 inch tube pan. Bake at 350 for 50 or 60 minutes. Invert pan to cool

DEVIL FOOD CAKE

    1 c. sour cream or 1 Tbsp. butter & 1 c. sour milk
    1 c. sugar
    1 egg, unbeaten
    Pinch of salt
    1 ½ c. flour
    1 tsp. baking soda, sifted with flour
    2 squares of chocolate
    1 ½ c. boiling water.

Boil water with chocolate and when thick, add to cake mixture. Beat. Pour into greased and flour-dusted cake pans. Back at 350° until a toothpick comes out clean.

ORANGE CAKE (MRS. KAMMER)

Cake Batter

    1 c. sugar
    ½ c. butter
    2 well beaten eggs
    1 c. sour milk
    2 c. flour
    1 tsp. baking powder
    1 tsp. baking soda in flour
    Pinch of salt

1 large orange, squeeze out juice and pulp and add ½ c. white sugar. Let stand, then take the rind of the orange and 1 c. raisins and put through grinder.

Mix cake batter and add the ground raisins and rind to the batter. When cake is about done, spread the orange juice and sugar over the top and put back in the oven to brown. Requires no frosting, orange juice and sugar form a coating.

APPLE SAUCE FRUIT CAKE

  3 c. hot apple sauce
  2 c. sugar
  1 lb. raisins
  1 tsp. nutmeg
  ¼ tsp. allspice
  4-½ c. flour
  1 c. shortening
  4 level tsp. baking soda
  1 lb. currants
  2 tsp. cinnamon
  ½ tsp. cloves
  Salt

Mix. Pour into greased and flour-dusted loaf pans. Bake in 2 loaves in a 350° oven.

SPICE CAKE

  1 c. brown sugar
  ¼ c. shortening
  ½ tsp. baking powder
  1 tsp. cloves
  1 tsp. cinnamon
  1 tsp. nutmeg
  1 tsp. allspice
  ½ tsp. salt
  1 c. raisins
  1 egg
  1 c. sour milk
  1 tsp. baking soda

Mix. Pour into greased and flour-dusted square pan. Bake in a 350° oven.

PORK CAKE (MRS. MANNEY)

> Pour 1 pt. strong coffee over 1 lb of fat salt pork, chopped fine.
>
> 1 tsp. baking soda, beaten in 1 c. of molasses until light.
>
> 2 c. brown sugar
>
> 1 tsp. nutmeg
>
> 1 Tbsp. cloves
>
> 6 c. flour
>
> 2 c. chopped nuts
>
> 1 lbs seeded raisins

Mix. Pour into greased and flour-dusted square pan. Bake in moderate (350°) oven for 1 hour.

RAISIN CAKE

Cover 1 ½ c. of raisins with boiling water and cook 20 minutes.

Cream 3/4 c. brown sugar with ¼ c. butter, add 1 ½ c. of flour with 1 tsp. baking soda sifted into flour. ½ c. raisins water, 1 egg beaten light, 1 tsp. nutmeg and cinnamon. Add raisins.

Mix. Pour into greased and flour-dusted square pan. Bake in moderate (350°) oven for 1 hour.

GRAHAM CRACKER CAKE

 1 large cup sugar
 ½ c. butter or shortening
 2 eggs
 2 tsp. baking powder
 1 c. graham crackers rolled fine
 1 c. flour
 1 c. milk
 1 c. nut meats

Cream butter and sugar. Add beaten yolks, sift flour and baking powder, add milk and graham crackers, then nut meats, beaten eggs whites, fold in. Pour into greased and flour-dusted square pan. Bake in moderate (350°) oven for 1 hour.

PECAN TEA CAKES (BERNICE LEE)

 2 eggs
 1 c. brown sugar
 ½ c. white flour
 ¼ tsp. salt
 ¼ tsp. baking powder
 Pecans

Bake in greased and flour-dusted pans for 15 min. in 350 degree oven. Watch and test.

CINNAMON CAKES

 ½ c. butter
 1 c. sugar
 2 eggs
 ¼ c. milk
 1 3/4 c. flour
 2 ½ tsp. baking powder
 1 tsp. cinnamon

Mix ingredients in the order given and bake in buttered gem tins.

INEXPENSIVE FRUIT CAKE (2 LOAVES) (MRS. RULE)

1 ½ c. seeded raisins, cut fine
1 ½ c. dates, chopped
5 Tbsp. shortening
3 c. flour
2 tsp. cinnamon
1 tsp. cloves
1 tsp. salt
1 tsp. baking soda
1 tsp. baking powder
1 c. chopped nuts
2 c. sugar
2 c. boiling water

Simmer slowly raisins, dates, 2 c. boiling water, sugar and shortening for 20 min. Sift flour, soda, spices and salt. Stir into cooled mixture, add nuts mixed with flour last. Bake in greased, well-floured pans or wax paper. 1 ½ hours in moderate (350 degrees) oven. 1 c. candied fruit may be added.

CRUMB CAKE

    2 c. brown sugar

    2 c. flour

    ½ c. butter

    Work these 3 things together and take out 1 c. of crumbs for top of cake.

    Take the rest & add 1 well-beaten egg.

    1 c. thick sour milk

    1 tsp. baking soda added to milk

    1 c. nut meats

    1 tsp. vanilla

    Pinch of salt

Put in greased & floured pan, put 1 c. of crumbs on top of cake. Bake in 350 degree oven.

WHITE FRUITCAKE (VERA OLSON)

1 c. shortening (scant)
1 c. sugar
½ c. honey
3 c. flour
¼ tsp. baking soda
2 tsp. baking powder
¼ tsp. salt
1 c. milk
grated rind of an orange
grated ring of a lemon
4 egg whites
1 c. white raisins
¼ c. citron
½ c. pineapple
1 c. cherries
1 c. walnuts

Cream shortening and sugar, add honey, beat well, sift 2 c. flour with soda, baking powder and salt. Use remaining flour for fruit and nuts, add sifted with other ingredients alternately to milk, beat well. Add grated rings. Beat egg whites until almost stiff, fold in, stir in rest of flour with fruit and nuts. Pour into greased and floured loaf pan. Bake in slow, 300 degree oven for 1 ½ hours.

Be scant on shortening.

WELLESLEY FUDGE CAKE

½ c. shortening

1 ½ c. sugar

2 eggs

2 c. of flour

1 tsp. baking soda

1 tsp. baking powder

½ tsp. salt

1 c. sour milk

½ c. cocoa

1/3 c. hot water

1 tsp. vanilla

Cream shortening, add the sugar and cream thoroughly. Add the well beaten eggs. Sift flour once before measuring, mix and sift flour, salt, soda and baking powder all together, and add to the first. Mix them alternately with sour milk. Mix the cocoa and hot water to form a paste, add to cake batter. Pour into greased floured tins and bake at 300 degrees for 40 minutes.

CHOCOLATE FUDGE ICING

2 sq. chocolate

1 ½ c. sugar

½ c. water

1 Tbsp. butter

¼ tsp. cream tartar or

1 Tbsp. light corn syrup

1 tsp. vanilla

2 Tbsp. of thick cream

Cut chocolate into small pieces, combine with sugar, water and butter and cream of tartar. Place on fire, cook without stirring until it forms a soft ball, when perfectly cool, add vanilla. Beat. If too thick, thin with cream. ½ c. nuts may be added.

UPSIDE DOWN CAKE

    3 egg yolks
    1 ¼ c. sugar
    2 c. flour
    3 egg whites
    1 c. brown sugar
    1 Tbsp. lemon juice
    ½ c. boiling water
    ¼ tsp. salt
    2 tsp. baking powder
    ¼ c. melted butter
    6 slices canned pineapple rings, cherries and nuts

Beat egg yolks until thick and lemon color. Add sugar and continue beating, add flour and boiling water, beat well. Beat egg white separately. Add salt and continue to beat egg whites until stiff. Add sifted flour and baking powder to egg yolks, alternately with egg whites.

Place melted butter in bottom of deep frying pan. Sprinkle brown sugar in bottom of pan.

Then place pineapple on top of brown sugar. Put cherry and/or nut in center of pineapple ring. Pour in cake mixture.

Bake slowly 1 hour at 325°.

Turn out while hot. Top with the glazed caramel mixture. Cool and serve with whipped cream.

SPICE CAKES

½ c. shortening
2 c. brown sugar
3 eggs
½ c. sour cream
1 c. sour milk
3 c. cake flour
1 ½ tsp. baking soda
1 Tbsp. cinnamon
½ tsp. nutmeg
1 c. chopped nuts
Raisins

Cream shortening and sugar. Add well beaten eggs, sift flour and measure, then sift flour, soda, cinnamon, and nutmeg together. Add alternately with sour milk and sour cream. Add chopped raisins last. Bake in greased and floured muffin tins 25 minutes in a moderate (350°) oven.

SOUR CREAM SPICE CAKES (GOOD)

1/3 c. fat
2 eggs
2 tsp. cinnamon
1 tsp. nutmeg
1 tsp. salt
½ c. black walnuts
1 tsp. baking soda
1 ½ c. dark brown sugar
1 c. thick sour cream
1 tsp. cloves
1 tsp. vanilla
1 c. raisins
2 ¼ c. flour

Cream the fat, add rest of ingredients and beat for 3 minutes. Half fill paper cups, arrange on baking sheet, bake 15 minutes in moderate (350°) oven. Cool and spread with frosting.

BANANA CREAM CAKE

½ c. Spry shortening
3/4 tsp. salt
½ tsp. ginger
1 ½ tsp. vanilla
1 c. sugar
2 eggs, unbeaten
2 tsp. baking powder
¼ tsp. baking soda
2 c. sifted flour
¼ c. sour milk
1 c. mashed bananas
1 c. heavy cream, whipped
¼ c. sifted confectionary sugar
¼ tsp. vanilla
2 bananas sliced

Blend Spry, salt, ginger and vanilla, add sugar gradually cream, add egg one at a time, beat well each time. Sift flour, baking powder and salt three times, add to creamed mixture, alternately with milk and bananas combined, mix until smooth. Bake in 8" greased layer pans in a moderate (350°) oven, 25 to 30 minutes.

Whip cream, add sugar & vanilla. Put layers together with whipped cream and bananas sliced. Put whipped cream on top of cake, garnish with overlapping rows of bananas.

CHOCOLATE PRUNE CAKE (MARGIE'S BIRTHDAY CAKE)

2 c. cooked prunes
2 c. shortening
1 ½ c. sugar
2 sq. (2 oz) bitter chocolate
3 eggs, well beaten
2 3/4 c. flour (pastry or cake)
4 tsp. baking powder
½ tsp. baking soda
½ tsp. salt
1 c. milk
1 tsp. vanilla

Pit prunes, cut into small pieces. Cream shortening and sugar, melt chocolate over hot water, add to creamed mixture, mix, add well beaten eggs, mix again. Sift flour with baking powder, soda and salt. Add alternately with milk (small amount at a time), add prunes and vanilla. Beat thoroughly. Put into three greased layer cake tins. Bake 25 or 30 minutes in a moderate (375 degree) oven. Put together with chocolate butter frosting.

RAISIN CAKE

Cover 1 ½ c. raisins with boiling water and cook for 20 minutes. Cream 3/4 c. brown sugar and ¼ c. butter. Add 1 ½ c. flour with 1 tsp. baking soda.

Then add the following ingredients:

½ raisin water

1 egg, beaten light

1 tsp. nutmeg

1 tsp. cinnamon, add raisins.

Mix and bake in moderate, 350 degree, oven until a toothpick comes out clean.

SPONGE CAKE (OLSON)

6 eggs, separated

1/8 tsp. salt

½ tsp. cream of tartar

1 ¼ c. sifted sugar

1 ½ Tbsp. lemon juice

1 ¼ c. sifted flour

Beat whites of eggs with salt until foamy, add cream of tartar and continue to beat until whites are stiff. Add sugar gradually, beating for three minutes until mixture holds shape. Beat egg yolks until light and creamy, add lemon juice, fold in whites. Fold in flour a little at a time. Pour into ungreased tin 10x5x3 loaf tin. Bake 1 hour and 10 minutes at 300 degrees. When done invert cake on rack, let cool before removing from pan.

RICH DEVIL'S CAKE (DOT)

1 ½ c. sugar
½ c. Crisco or Spry shortening
2 eggs
2 sq. of chocolate
1 tsp. baking soda
1 c. sour milk or buttermilk
pinch of salt
1 tsp. vanilla
2 c. flour (cake flour)

Cream shortening and sugar, add well-beaten eggs, cut of chocolate in cup, fill to 2/3 mark with hot water add soda to chocolate just before putting in cake. Add flour and milk alternately and vanilla. Bake 350 degrees for 30 or 35 minutes.

CHERRY CAKE (MRS. RULE)

½ c. butter
1 ½ c. sugar
3 c. cake flour
3 tsp. baking powder
½ tsp. salt
3 egg whites beaten stiffly
6 oz jar Maraschino cherries

Cup of juice, add water to make cupful. Cut cherries fine. ½ c. nut meats. Cream butter, add sugar. Sift flour, baking powder and salt add to creamed mixture alternately with cherry juice. Add nuts and cherries, cut fine. Add beaten egg whites last. Bake 30 to 35 min in 350 degree oven.

PICNIC CAKE (ADAH SHIMER)

½ c. shortening (part butter for flavor)

1 ½ c. sugar

2 eggs

2 ½ c. sifted flour

3 tsp. baking powder

½ tsp. salt

1 c. milk

1 tsp. vanilla

12 marshmallows (1/4 lb)

½ c. brown sugar

1 c. nut meats, chopped

Cream shortening, add sugar gradually cream until fluffy, add eggs one at a time, beating after each, sift flour, baking powder and salt together. Add to mixture alternately with milk. Add vanilla. Pour into greased pan (floured) cut marshmallows crosswise and arrange on top of cake. Mix brown sugar and nuts. Sprinkle over top of cake. Bake 50 or 45 minutes in 350 degree oven.

BANANA CAKE

1 c. sugar

½ c. shortening

Pinch of salt

2 eggs

3 bananas, mashed fine

5 Tbsp. sour milk

1 tsp. baking soda

1 3/4 c. flour

Mix ingredients in order given. Bake 35 to 40 minutes in 325 or 350 degree oven.

CHEESE CAKE (SERVES 9)

FILLING

    3 eggs

    3 packages cream cheese

    1 tsp. vanilla

    2 c. sugar

    1 ½ tsp. flour (If not stiff enough, try Tbsp. flour)

    2/3 c. whipping cream

CRUST

    1 ½ c. graham cracker crumbs

    ½ c. chopped nuts

    1/3 c. sugar

    2 tsp. melted butter

Filling: Separate eggs. Beat egg yolks. Beat cheese into yolks add vanilla, sugar and flour. Whip cream and fold into cheese mixture. Pour cheese mixture onto graham cracker crust.

Crust: Mix together graham cracker crumbs and nuts. 1/3 c. sugar and butter. Reserve 1/3 c. for the top. Line cake pan with cracker mixture. Put in filling in pan put on cracker topping and bake slow at 300 degrees for 1 hour or a little more. You may omit the nuts.

DATE CAKE (OLIN)

    1 c. sugar
    ½ c. butter
    2 Sq. chocolate
    2 eggs
    1 c. sour milk
    1 tsp. baking powder
    1 tsp. Vanilla
    1 apple or raisins
    1 tsp. baking soda
    1 ½ c. flour
    1 Package dates
    1 c. nut meats

Mix. Pour into greased and flour-dusted square pan. Bake in moderate (350°) oven until a toothpick comes out clean.

APPLE SAUCE CAKE (FLETCHER)

Sift Together:

    2 ½ c. flour
    1 c. sugar
    2 tsp. baking soda
    1 tsp. salt
    1 Tbsp. cocoa
    Spices to Taste

Add:

1 ½ c. apple sauce

½ c. shortening

1 c. raisins

1 c. chopped nuts

Mix. Pour into greased and flour-dusted square pan. Bake in moderate (350°) oven until a toothpick comes out clean.

DROP CAKES

1 ½ c. brown sugar

½ c. lard

½ c. butter

3 eggs beaten light (add last)

2 c. flour

1 tsp. baking soda dissolved in 2 tsp. hot water

1 c. dates

1 c. nut meats

Mix dry ingredients. Mix in wet ingredients.

Author's note: No cooking method listed, so...perhaps pour into greased and flour-dusted square pan. Bake in moderate (350°) oven until a toothpick comes out clean.

ADAH'S WHITE CAKE (GOOD)

 1 ½ c. white sugar (sift after measuring)
 2 rounded Tbsp. butter
 3 egg whites
 1 ½ c. cold water
 3 c. Swansdown cake flour, measured after sifting
 4 tsp. baking powder (3 oz calumet)
 1 tsp. vanilla
 few drops of almond extract
 pinch of salt

Cream butter and sugar. Add dry ingredients, which have been sifted four times, with the cold water a little at a time. Beat well. Then fold in well beaten egg whites. Bake in 350 degree oven.

PINEAPPLE CAKE (MRS. GRAHAM)

 2 ½ c. sifted flour
 3 tsp. baking powder
 ½ c. butter
 1 ¼ c. sugar
 Whites of 4 eggs
 3/4 c. pineapple juice

Sift flour and baking powder together 3 times. Cream butter and sugar, add flour, moistening with pineapple juice. Add well beaten egg whites last. Bake in 2 cake pans (greased and floured) in a slow (350°) oven.

Honey Chocolate Cake (Helen Manny)

3 sqs unsweetened chocolate, melted
2/3 c. honey
1 3/4 c. sifted flour
1 tsp. baking soda
½ c. shortening
1 tsp. vanilla
2/3 c. water
3/4 tsp. salt
½ c. sugar
2 eggs

Blend chocolate and honey (cool to lukewarm). Sift flour once, measure, add soda and salt. Sift together 3 times. Cream sugar and shortening. Add chocolate and honey mixture, vanilla, add eggs one at a time. Add flour alternately with water. Pour into greased and floured square cake pan. Bake in moderate (350°) oven, 30 to 35 minutes.

Prize Burnt Sugar Cake

All ingredients must be at room temperature.

MELT: ½ c. sugar in skillet over low heat until dark brown; stir constantly.

ADD GRADUALLY: 3/4 c. scalded milk, stirring until all caramel is dissolved. Cool.

POUR: into measuring cup and add enough milk to bring caramel mixture to 1 level cup.

SIFT TOGETHER: 2 cups sifted flour, 3 tsp. double-acting baking powder (or 4 ½ tsp. single-acting), 1 tsp. salt, 3/4 c. sugar.

ADD: ½ cup vegetable shortening, 2/3 cup caramel mixture.

BEAT: for 2 minutes until batter is well-blended and glossy. (If electric mixer is used, beat at medium speed for same period of time.)

ADD: ½ c. caramel mixture, 2 eggs, unbeaten, and 1 tsp. vanilla.

BEAT: for two minutes.

POUR: into two, lightly greased, floured, 8" layer cake pans.

BAKE: at 350 degrees for 30 to 35 minutes.

FROST: with caramel frosting

CARAMEL FROSTING FOR PRIZE BURNT SUGAR CAKE

COMBINE: 1 c. firmly packed brown sugar, 1 c. granulated sugar, and 2/3 c. cream.

COOK: until a little syrup dropped in cold water forms a soft ball.

REMOVE: from heat and cool to lukewarm.

ADD: ½ tsp. vanilla, 1/8 tsp. salt.

BEAT: until thick and proper consistency for spreading.

COCOA VELVET CAKE

SIFT TOGETHER IN A BOWL:
> 1 3/4 c. sifted flour
> 1 1/4 to 1 3/4 tsp. Baking Powder
> ½ tsp. baking soda
> 1 tsp. salt
> 1 ½ c. sugar
> 6 Tbsp. cocoa

ADD:

2/3 c. vegetable shortening

1 c. buttermilk or sour milk (1 Tbsp. vinegar or lemon juice in 1 c. milk)

Make sure all ingredients are at room temperature. Shortening should be soft, not melted. Pre-heat oven to 350 degrees. Grease and flour two 8" cake pans or one 8 ½" square pan. Sift flour before measuring. Measure all ingredients before starting to mix.

Beat vigorously with spoon (up and over motion) or mix with electric mixer on slow to medium speed for 2 minutes by clock. Scrape bowl frequently.

ADD:

½ to 2/3 c. eggs (unbeaten)

¼ tsp. Red Coloring

Continue beating 2 minutes, scraping bowl frequently. Pour into prepared (greased and floured) pans. Bake layers 30 to 35 minutes (or bake square 45 to 50 minutes) in moderate (350°) oven. Cool.

Use fluffy white or creamy chocolate icing.

ORANGE HONEY CAKE (HELEN MANNY)

2 c. sifted flour
3 ½ tsp. baking powder
½ c. shortening
2/3 c. honey
½ c. orange juice
2 egg whites, stiffly beaten
3/4 tsp. salt
½ c. sugar
2 egg yolks

Sift flour once, measure, add baking powder, salt and sift 3 times. Cream shortening and sugar. Add honey then egg yolks and beat. Add flour alternately with orange juice. Beat until smooth. Fold in egg whites. Bake 30 to 35 minutes in a 350 degree oven.

ORANGE GINGER BREAD (GIRL'S CLUB)

2 c. flour
½ c. molasses
½ c. syrup
½ c. melted fat
½ c. boiling water
½ tsp. ginger
½ tsp. cinnamon
2 tsp. baking soda
1 orange, grated rind and juice
Pinch of salt

Mix all ingredients together. Bake in muffin tins in a moderate (350°) oven.

SAUCE:

juice of 1 orange and 1 lemon
1 ½ c. sugar
2 c. water
2 Tbsp. cornstarch heaping

Add 1 Tbsp. of butter and boil until thick.

DATE CUP CAKES

½ c. sifted flour
½ tsp. baking powder
¼ tsp. salt
½ c. chopped walnuts
½ c. chopped dates
2 eggs
½ tsp. vanilla
1 c. brown sugar, firmly packed

Sift flour, baking powder, and salt onto paper. Add dates and set aside. Beat eggs in mixing bowl. Add vanilla, then gradually beat in the brown sugar. Sift in flour and fruit, and mix well. Fill well-greased tin muffin pans not more than 2/3 full and bake in moderately hot oven, 375°, about 15 minutes. Cool on rack, then store tightly covered. Do not frost.

CHOCOLATE CAKE

    1 ½ c. sifted Swansdown Cake Flour

    1 tsp. cream of tartar

    3/4 tsp. baking soda

    1 tsp. salt

    1 ½ c. sugar

    ½ c. shortening

    2 eggs unbeaten

    3 Sq. Baker's unsweetened chocolate, melted

    1 tsp. vanilla

With butter or lard use 1 c. milk, with vegetable shortening use 1 c. milk plus 2 Tbsp.

Combine flour, salt, cream of tartar and soda. Sift three times. Cream shortening, add sugar gradually, add eggs one at a time, beat well after each, add flour alternately with milk, small amount at a time. Beat after each addition. Add chocolate and vanilla. Bake in two 9" layer pans in 350 degree oven for 30 minutes.

RIBBON ICE BOX CAKES

    Prepare 1 package cherry Jell-O, let cool

Into loaf pan, place layer of graham crackers, fit tightly. Spread over them the following mixture:

    ½ c. powdered sugar

    1 egg yolk, beaten

    ¼ c. walnut meats

    ¼ c. butter

    ¼ c. crushed, drained pineapple

Fold in stiffly beaten egg whites. Put in 3 layers of crackers, 2 layers of mixture, and crackers on top.

When Jell-O has begun to set, pour ½ over crackers. Whip remainder to froth and pour over top. Let stand in cool place overnight.

Slice and serve with whipped cream and cherries on top.

GINGER BREAD (DAHLIA)

Sift together ¼ c. sugar, 1 c. sifted flour, 1 tsp. baking soda, 1 tsp. ginger, 1 tsp. cinnamon, ½ tsp. salt.

Add to dry ingredients ¼ c. of molasses, ¼ c. sweet milk, ¼ c. of sour milk and beat 2 minutes. Add 1 well-beaten egg, ¼ c. of melted butter. Beat again for 3 or 4 minutes. Bake in greased 8" pan in a 350 degree oven for 25 or 30 minutes.

ANGEL FOOD (MYRTLE)

    1 c. cake flour
    1 ¼ c. egg whites (8-10 eggs)
    1 ¼ tsp. cream of tartar
    Pinch of salt
    1 tsp. flavoring (orange, lemon, vanilla or almond)

Sift flour and ¾ c. sugar. Sift four times.

Whip egg whites. Add salt. When frothy, add cream of tartar and continue whipping until stiff. Fold in ¾ c. sugar, gradually, 1 heaping Tbsp. at a time. Then sift in 1 or 2 Tbsp. flour at a time and flavoring. Place wax paper in bottom of cake pan.

Bake 1 hour 10 min at 325°. Turn bottom side up until cool.

CUSTARD SAUCE FOR ANGEL FOOD

        5 egg yolks
        1/3 c. sugar
        1 c. cream

Heat until thick in double boiler. Can add nuts, vanilla, grated rind and juice of an orange.

APPLESAUCE CUPCAKES

        1/3 c. margarine
        2 c. sifted flour
        1 tsp. baking soda
        ¼ tsp. salt
        1 tsp. cinnamon
        ½ tsp. cloves
        ½ c. seedless raisins
        ½ c. chopped nut meats
        1 c. sugar
        1 c. unsweetened applesauce

Sift flour, soda, salt and spices together. Mix in raisins and nut meats. Cream margarine. Add sugar, creaming well. Add egg and beat until mixture is fluffy. Add applesauce alternately with dry ingredients, adding dry ingredients first and last. Rub muffin tins with margarine. Fill 2/3 full with batter. Bake in moderate oven, 375° for 20 – 25 minutes. Cool and frost with Snowy White Frosting.

Snowy White Frosting for Applesauce Cupcakes

>   1/3 c. margarine
>   ½ tsp. vanilla
>   1 ¼ c. sifted confectioners' sugar
>   1 Tbsp. milk

Cream margarine until soft and fluffy. Beat in vanilla. Add confectioners' sugar gradually, alternating with milk. Beat until smooth and creamy. Greater volume will be achieved by machine-mixed frosting than by hand.

Mocha Frosting

Use ingredients list from Snowy White Frosting except sift 1/3 c. sifted cocoa with confectioners' sugar. Substitute 2 Tbsp. very strong coffee for milk.

Holiday Fruit Cake

Cut the following fine. Dredge in ¼ c. flour. Add Nuts:

¼ lb citron

¼ lb candied orange peel

¼ lb candied lemon peel

½ lb candied cherries

¼ lb candied pineapple

½ lb dark seedless raisins

½ lb white seedless raisins

¼ lb enriched

flour

¼ lb California nuts (walnuts) chopped

¼ lb pecans

1 c. shortening

2 c. brown sugar

4 large eggs (1 c.)

½ c. grape jelly

½ c. grape juice

2 3/4 c. sifted flour

1 tsp. baking powder

1 tsp. salt

1 tsp. cinnamon

1 tsp. allspice

½ tsp. nutmeg

½ tsp. cloves

Cream shortening & sugar. Add eggs, beat well. Soften jelly, combine with grape juice, add sifted dry ingredients alternately with grape juice mixture, beat thoroughly. Pour batter over floured fruit & nut mixture.

Pour into wax paper lined tins, 3 ½ x 1 ½ loaf tins. Allow ½" to extend above all sides of pans. Bake in very slow (350°) oven 250 degrees three to 4 hours. Place pan containing 2 c. water on bottom shelf of oven to give greater volume to cakes.

Cool, brush with hot corn syrup, decorate with orange and lemon slices. Makes 6 lbs.

PINEAPPLE UPSIDE-DOWN CAKE (OLIN)

Use any kind of white cake in iron skillet, well buttered.

>1 c. brown sugar
>Pineapple
>Butter
>1 c. sugar
>3 c. flour
>3 tsp. baking powder
>Pinch salt

Sift dry ingredients together. Add:

>2 eggs
>2 c. milk

Mix in 6 Tbsp. of melted shortening. Put topping into pan, then cake batter and bake at 350° until toothpick comes out clean.

BROWN SUGAR CAKE (DOROTHY RUSSELL)

        2 c. brown sugar
        ½ c. shortening
        ¼ tsp. salt
        2 eggs
        1 c. sour milk
        1 tsp. baking soda
        1 tsp. cinnamon
        ½ tsp. nutmeg
        ½ tsp. cloves
        2 c. flour
        1 c. raisins
        1 tsp. lemon or vanilla

Mix batter, pour into a greased and floured square pan, and bake at 350° until toothpick comes out clean.

YELLOW CAKE (GOOD)

Sift Together:

        2 c. sifted cake flour
        1 1/3 c. sugar
        3 tsp. baking powder
        1 tsp. salt

Then add:

        1/3 c. spry or shortening
        3/4 c. milk.

Add:

        1 tsp. vanilla

1/3 tsp. lemon added to milk, beat 2 minutes

6 egg yolks, beat 2 minutes

Pour batter into a greased and floured pan. Bake 30 minutes in 350 degree oven.

FROSTING FOR YELLOW CAKE

Beat 2 minutes:

> 3 Tbsp. butter (softened)
> 1 c. brown sugar

Add ¼ c. cream. Put on stove, stir until it boils. Then cover and boil up. Cool. Add 1 ½ c. powdered sugar and flavoring.

ORANGE GINGER BREAD (GIRL'S CLUB)

> 2 c. flour
> ½ c. molasses
> ½ c. syrup
> ½ c. melted fat
> ½ c. boiling water
> ½ tsp. ginger
> ½ tsp. cinnamon
> 2 tsp. baking soda
> 1 orange grated rind & juice
> Dash of Salt

Mix all ingredients together. Bake in muffin tins in a moderate (350°) oven until a toothpick comes out clean.

SAUCE

BOIL:

Juice of 1 orange
Juice of 1 lemon
1 ½ c. sugar
2 ½ c. water
2 Tbsp. (heaping) of cornstarch.

After boiling, add butter until desired consistency.

TOASTED ALMOND CAKE (MARGE SCHROEDER)

 2 c. Gold Medal flour (sifted)
 1 ¼ c. sugar
 3 ¼ tsp. double acting baking powder
 1 tsp. salt

ADD:

 ½ c. Crisco
 7/8 c. (3/4 c. plus 2 Tbsp) milk
 1 ½ tsp. vanilla

Beat at low or medium speed for 2 minutes. Scrap sides and bottom often.

Add ½ c. unbeaten egg whites (3 large egg whites).

Beat 2 more minutes, scraping bowl often.

Pour batter into greased and floured cake pans. Bake in 375 degree oven for 25 to 30 minutes.

DOUBLE CHOCOLATE CAKE (MARGE SCHROEDER)
SIFT TOGETHER:

 1 3/4 c. Gold Medal flour
 1 ½ c. sugar
 1 ¼ tsp. double acting baking powder
 ½ tsp. baking soda
 1 tsp. salt

Then ADD:

½ c. vegetable shortening

1 c. milk

1 tsp. vanilla

Mix with electric egg beater on low to medium speed for 2 minutes, scrap bottom often.

Add ½ to 2/3 c. unbeaten egg (2 large), 2 sq. of unsweetened chocolate (2 oz)*, ½ tsp. red food coloring. Mix 2 minutes more.

Pour into greased & floured pans. Bake 375 degree oven 30 to 35 minutes.

* You can use 6 Tbsp. cocoa in place of chocolate if you increase shortening 1 Tbsp. Sift cocoa with dry ingredients.

TREASURE CHEST CAKE (VERY GOOD)

Boil until thick:

1 c. raisins

1 c. dates

1 c. nut meats

Little water

Then mix with juice.

3/4 c. orange juice and grated rind

Let the above mixture stand till ready for cake batter. Use half for cake and other half mixed with powdered sugar for frosting on cake. When cake is cool, frost.

2 c. sifted flour

1 tsp. baking powder

1 tsp. baking soda

1 tsp. each spices: cinnamon, allspice, nutmeg

½ c. shortening

1 c. sugar

1 egg, well beaten

1 c. sour milk or butter milk

1 tsp. vanilla

Sift dry ingredients 3 times, cream shortening and sugar until fluffy. Add beaten egg and vanilla, add sour milk alternately with dry ingredients. Then add ½ fruit mixture. Bake in moderate (350°) oven.

Mix remaining fruit with powdered sugar to frost cake.

HOT MILK SPONGE CAKE

1 c. sifted cake flour

1 tsp. Calumet baking powder

3 eggs

1 c. sugar

2 tsp. lemon juice

6 Tbsp. hot milk

Sift flour once, measure, add baking powder, and sift together three times. Beat eggs until very thick and light (nearly white, about 10 minutes of beating). Add sugar gradually, beat constantly. Add lemon juice. Fold in flour a little at a time until all is added. Add milk mixing quickly until batter is smooth.

Bake in ungreased tube pan in 350 degree oven for 35 minutes or until done. Can bake in two lightly greased pans 8x8x2 in 350 degree oven for 25 minutes.

Sift powdered sugar on top, cut in squares, serve as a dessert. Top with fresh berry topping.

SPANISH BUN CAKE (MRS. KRUSE AT THE LODGE)

   2 c. brown sugar
   ½ c. butter or shortening
   1 c. butter milk
   4 well beaten eggs
   2 ½ c. flour
   1 tsp. cloves
   2 tsp. cinnamon
   1 tsp. allspice
   ½ tsp. nutmeg
   1 tsp. baking soda
   ¼ tsp. salt
   1 tsp. vanilla & lemon
   1 c. raisins

Mix batter, pour into a greased and floured pan, and bake in moderate oven at 350° for 1 hour or until done.

CANDY

DIVINITY FUDGE

Cook until hard ball stage:

> 3 c. white sugar
> ½ c. white syrup
> ¾ c. water

Then slowly add to boiled mixture:

> 2 eggs whites, beaten stiff

Beat.

Add:

> Piece of butter (approx. 1 Tbsp)
> 1 c. of nut meats
> 1 tsp. vanilla

After adding nuts, butter & flavoring, drop on buttered plates.

SEA FOAM

> ½ c. brown sugar
> 1 c. white sugar
> 2/3 c. water
> 1 egg white
> 1/8 tsp. salt
> 1 tsp. vanilla

Boil sugar and water without stirring, until fine threads form when dribbled from spoon.

Pour into beaten egg whites.

Beat until mixture thickens.

Add rest of ingredients and drop from spoon onto waxed paper.

Top with nuts or dates.

MARJORIE'S CANDY

1 ½ c. sugar
½ c. sweet milk
1 Tbsp. butter
2 squares of chocolate, melted
1 tsp. vanilla
½ c. walnut meats

Mix and let cool.

CHRISTMAS DIXIES

2 c. sugar
1 c. dark brown sugar
1 ½ c. water
3 Tbsp. butter
1 tsp. vanilla
½ tsp. lemon extract
½ c. toasted cocoanut
½ c. pecans
½ c. candied cherries
½ c. candied pineapple

Boil sugars, water and butter. Stir frequently until soft ball stage (a soft ball forms when a drop is dribbled into cold water). Remove from fire. Let stand 20 minutes. Add extracts and beat until creamy. Add rest of ingredients and drop portions from tip of spoon onto wax paper to cool.

CARAMEL CORN BALLS (DON VADER)

Approx. 4 or 5 Qts. Of popped corn
1 c. brown sugar
1 Tbsp. butter
¼ c. water

Boil sugar, butter and water for about 8 min. or until soft ball stage.

Pour mixture over popped corn.

Form into balls.

POPCORN BALLS (ADAH SHIMER)

1 ¼ c. white Karo syrup
1 c. sugar
1 Tbsp. water
1 Tbsp. vinegar
1 tsp. butter
1 tsp. vanilla

Mix all together except vanilla. Boil until drops form a ball in cold water.

Pour syrup over popcorn. Mix well.

Let stand a few minutes until syrup starts to cool. Grease hands good and form mixture into balls. Press firmly into falls and set aside to cool

SEA FOAM

2 c. brown sugar
½ c. water

Boil sugar and water until threads form when dribbled from tip of spoon.

Pour over beaten white of 1 egg.

Beat until stiff enough to drop by teaspoons on a greased sheet.

OLIN'S SEA FOAM

    2 c. white sugar
    ½ c. light or dark syrup
    ½ c. cold water

Boil ingredients until drops form a hard ball when dripped into cold water.

Beat the whites of 2 eggs stiff. Add a little of boiled mixture a little at a time. Beat until cold.

Add dates, nuts, vanilla.

Drop by teaspoonful on greased pan.

PEANUT CANDY

    2 c. brown sugar
    ¾ c. hot water
    Pinch of salt
    ½ c. chopped peanuts

Boil sugar, water and other ingredients (except peanuts) until a drop forms a soft ball when dripped into cold water. Remove from fire and beat. Add chopped peanuts and beat until thick and creamy.

Drop onto waxed paper with teaspoon.

PEANUT BRITTLE

    2 c. sugar
    1 level tsp. soda
    1 c. chopped peanuts

Put sugar in hot frying pan and stir constantly over hot fire until melted. Add peanuts with soda stirred through them. Mix and empty at once into a large platter which has been well greased.

When cool break apart.

COCOANUT CANDY

    2 ½ c. granulated sugar
    1 c. cream or milk
    Butter the size of an egg
    1 Tsp. vanilla
    1 c. cocoanut.

Boil sugar and cream for 20 minutes.

Add remaining ingredients. Beat well. Pour into a buttered tin. Let cool.

TAFFY

    3 c. white sugar
    1 c. corn syrup
    Pinch of salt
    ¼ c. water
    1 tsp. vinegar
    1 tsp. butter

Mix until a small bit cracks in cold water. Add ¼ tsp. soda and stir.

Just before removing from stove, add 1 tsp. vanilla.

Pour into buttered pan and cool. Watch so it doesn't get too cool—just cool enough to work with. Butter hands and stretch until it gets glossy.

MRS. NELSON'S FUDGE

    1 c. sugar

    2 squares chocolate

    1 c. rich milk

    1 Tbsp. syrup or honey

    ½ tsp. salt

    "All the butter you can afford" (1 stick?)

    1 tsp. vanilla

    Chopped nuts

Mix. Add vanilla, then add nuts last.

FUDGE

    6 Tbsp. cream cheese (3oz package), creamed

    2 c. sifted confectioners' sugar

    2 ea 1 oz. squares of melted, unsweetened chocolate

    ¼ tsp. vanilla

    Dash of salt

    ½ c. chopped pecans

Slowly blend sugar into creamed cream cheese. Then thoroughly mix in the melted chocolate, vanilla, salt, and pecans.

Press into a well-greased pan and place in refrigerator 15 min or until firm.

Can add candied fruit, too, for a change.

COOKIES

OATMEAL COOKIE (MORE LIKE CANDY)

In a saucepan mix:

> 2 c. sugar
> ½ c. butter or shortening
> ½ c. cocoa
> ½ c. milk

Bring to a boil quickly, reduce heat to medium boil for 3 or 4 minutes or until a little dropped in cold water forms a soft ball.

Remove from heat, add 3 c. rolled oats (quick), ½ c. nut meats and vanilla. Drop by spoonful on wax paper. Let cool, pack in cookie jar.

CHERRY COCOANUT BARS (DOROTHY PFIELSTICKER)

PASTRY:
> 1 c. flour
> ½ c. butter
> 3 Tbsp. powdered sugar

TOP:

2 eggs, slightly beaten
1 c. sugar
¼ c. flour
½ tsp. baking powder
½ tsp. salt
3 c. chopped nuts
½ c. chopped cherries (maraschino)
½ c. cocoanut

Press pastry into greased and floured 5x10x2" pan and bake at 350 degrees for 20 minutes or 30 minutes.

Stir rest of ingredients into eggs. Spread on top of pastry and return to oven for another 25 minutes at 350 degrees. Cool and cut into bars.

Dorothy Pfielsticker's Congo Bars

2 3/4 c. sifted flour
2 ½ tsp. baking powder
½ tsp. salt
2/3 c. melted shortening
2 ¼ c. brown sugar
3 eggs
1 tsp. vanilla
1 c. nut meats
1 pkg chocolate chips

Melt shortening, add sugar, mix. Add 1 egg at a time. Add dry ingredients, put into greased baking pan and bake at 350 degrees about 30 minutes.

SOUR CREAM DROP COOKIES

½ c. shortening
1 ½ c. brown sugar
1 tsp. soda
½ tsp. salt
2 eggs
1 c. thick sour cream
2 ½ c. sifted flour
1 tsp. vanilla
½ tsp. baking powder
2/3 c. chopped walnuts

Cream shortening and sugar. Add eggs. Mix well.

Add sifted dry ingredients alternately with sour cream.

Blend in vanilla and chopped nuts.

Drop by teaspoonfuls on greased baking sheet. Bake at 350° for 10-12 minutes.

Frost with icing below.

SOUR CREAM DROP COOKIE ICING

6 Tbsp. butter
1 ½ c. powdered sugar
1 tsp. vanilla

Melt and brown butter. Add powdered sugar and vanilla. Blend in a few drops of hot water until icing is spreading consistency.

Molasses Sugar Cookies

¾ c. shortening
1 c. sugar
¼ c. molasses
1 egg
2 tsp. baking soda
2 c. sifted flour
½ tsp. cloves
½ tsp. ginger
1 tsp. cinnamon
½ tsp. salt

Melt shortening in 3 or 4 qt. saucepan over low heat. Remove from heat and cool. Then add sugar, molasses, and egg. Beat well.

Sift together flour, soda, spices, and salt.

Add dry mixture to wet ingredients. Mix well and chill thoroughly.

Form 1" balls. Roll in granulated sugar and place on a greased cookie sheet 2" apart.

Bake in moderate oven at 375° for 8-10 minutes.

Makes about 4 dozen.

Gordon's Cookies

1 egg yolk
6 Tbsp. butter or margarine
6 Tbsp. powdered sugar
Flour (try about 10 Tbsp, add more if needed).

Mix, drop onto greased cookie sheet and bake at 375°.

FRUIT COOKIES (MRS. MacDONALD)

        2 c. brown sugar
        2 eggs
        1 c. shortening (part butter)
        ½ c. sour milk
        1 tsp. baking soda
        1 tsp. salt
        1 c. fruit (candied)
        ½ c. dates, cut fine
        ½ c. nuts, cut fine
        3 ½ c. flour

Mix, drop onto greased cookie sheet and bake at 375°.

MRS. AKERHAUGEN'S WHITE COOKIES

        1 ½ c. sugar
        1 c. shortening, part butter
        1 c. sour cream
        2 eggs
        1 tsp. baking soda in boiling water
        1 tsp. vanilla
        ½ tsp. salt
        Flour (approx 3 cups)
        1 tsp. baking powder sifted into flour

Mix, drop onto greased cookie sheet and bake at 375°.

XMAS COOKIES (MRS. HENRY VERHAGEN)

1 ½ c. sugar, white
¼ tsp. salt
1 c. shortening, part butter
3 eggs
½ c. dates
1 tsp. baking soda dissolved in ¼ c. hot water

Mix dates, soda & water.

½ tsp. cinnamon
½ lb nut meats
1 package chocolate chips
½ c. cocoanut
½ c. mashed green cherries
½ c. red cherries
3 c. flour
1 tsp. vanilla

Mix in the order given and drop by tsp. onto greased cookie sheet. Bake in 325 degree oven about 15 minutes.

CHRISTMAS COOKIES (MRS. ROSE VERHAGEN)

    3 lbs brown sugar

    6 eggs

    1 pint hot water

    1 c. molasses

    1 lb shelled walnuts

    3 tsp. baking soda

    1 tsp. cinnamon

    ½ tsp. cloves

Flour to stiffen, and let stand for three days. Roll and bake.

LOVELY COOKIES (MRS. OLSON) *AMY'S FAVORITE

    3 c. flour

    1 c. shortening, part butter

    ½ tsp. baking soda

    ½ tsp. baking powder

    ½ tsp. salt

Mix like pie crust, really good. In a separate bowl, beat 2 eggs. Add 1 c. (large) of sugar, any flavoring. Add this to first mixture.

These cookies can be rolled out or put in cookie press. Cook on greased cookie sheet and bake at 375° but do not let get brown.

STATE PRIZE WHEELS (MRS. OLSON)

- 2 c. brown sugar
- 1 c. shortening
- 3 eggs
- 1 tsp. cinnamon
- 1 tsp. baking soda
- ½ tsp. salt
- 4 c. flour
- 1 tsp. vanilla

FILLING:

- ½ lb dates, cut up
- ½ c. water
- ½ c. sugar

Boil until thick and add1 c. nuts.

Roll dough to ½ " thick. Spread on filling and roll like a jelly roll. Chill and slice. Bake 8 to 10 minutes in 375 degree oven. Makes 4 doz.

MEXICAN WEDDING COOKIES (MRS. OLSON)

- 1 c. butter
- 6 Tbsp. powdered sugar
- 2 c. cake flour (sifted)
- 1 tsp. vanilla
- 1 c. chopped nuts

Roll a spoonful of dough into a ball. Place on greased cookie sheet. Bake in 375 degree oven until done. When cool, roll in powdered sugar.

SONJA HENIE COOKIES

½ c. shortening
½ c. brown sugar
1 egg yolk
1 c. flour
1 c. shopped pecans, put ½ in dough, roll in rest

Cream shortening and sugar. Add egg yolks, beat well. Add pecans and flour. Make small balls, dip in egg white and chopped pecans. Press flat with fork. Bake (not too fast), e.g. 350° oven.

DATE COOKIES

    2 c. brown sugar
    1 c. shortening, ½ of that should be butter
    3 eggs beaten
    1 tsp. baking soda (in a little hot water)
    ½ tsp. salt
    1 tsp. vanilla
    3 ½ c. flour

DATE FILLING:

    About 2 c. dates, cut fine
    2 Tbsp. sugar
    ½ c. water

Filling: cook until thick.

Cookies: Drop small mound of dough on cookie sheet, put some date filling on top and a smaller dab of dough on top of the filling. Bake, not too fast, e.g. 350° oven.

BUTTER BALLS (MRS. OLSON)

    1 c. butter or shortening
    2/3 c. sugar
    1 egg
    1 tsp. salt
    1 tsp. vanilla
    1 ½ c. ground Brazil nuts
    1 3/4 c. flour

Drop from tsp. onto greased cookie sheet, bake in 350° oven.

CINNAMON COOKIES (MRS. OLSON)

    3/4 c. butter or shortening
    1 c. brown sugar
    1 egg
    1 tsp. vanilla
    1 tsp. baking soda
    2 c. sifted flour

Make little balls, roll in cinnamon and sugar. Flatten with fork. Bake, 2 " apart on sheet, for 10 to 12 minutes.

RICH OATMEAL COOKIES

    2 c. brown sugar
    1 c. shortening
    3 c. ground oatmeal
    2 c. flour
    1 tsp. baking soda
    1 tsp. vanilla
    3 eggs, well beaten

Mix dry ingredients thoroughly, add melted butter or shortening, add eggs. Roll into small ball with hands and bake on greased cookie sheet in 375 degree oven.

SPICE NUT COOKIES (ICE BOX)

    1 c. shortening
    2 c. brown sugar
    3 eggs
    2 Tbsp. cream or milk
    ½ tsp. salt
    2 tsp. cinnamon
    1 tsp. cloves
    1 tsp. nutmeg
    1 tsp. chopped nuts
    4 ½ c. flour
    1 ½ tsp. baking soda

Make in roll, put in refrigerator. When hard, slice and bake in 375 degree oven.

ICE BOX GINGER COOKIES

    ½ c. fat
    ¼ c. boiling water
    ½ c. brown sugar
    ½ c. molasses
    1 tsp. baking soda
    3 c. flour
    ½ tsp. ginger
    1/3 tsp. nutmeg

Pour water over the fat, add sugar and molasses, mix the baking soda, flour, salt, spices and add to first mixture. Place in roll. Chill, and slice thin. Bake in hot (450°) oven.

MOLASSES COOKIES (MRS. OLSON)

CREAM together until fluffy:

3/4 c. shortening
1 c. brown sugar
¼ c. molasses
1 egg

SIFT together:

2 ¼ c. sifted flour
2 tsp. baking soda
½ tsp. salt
1 tsp. ginger
1 tsp. cinnamon
½ tsp. cloves

After mixing dry ingredients, stir into creamed mixture and blend well. Form into small balls, bake on greased cookie sheet for 10 minutes in 375 degree oven.

SALLY ANNS

1 c. brown sugar
1 c. white sugar
1 c. lard or 1 c. butter or 1 lb oleo
1 c. flour
1 tsp. nutmeg
1 tsp. vanilla
1 tsp. baking soda
½ tsp. salt
3 eggs
1 c. nut meats

Stir together then add 4 cups flour. Make into two rolls. Chill overnight. In morning, slice and bake in 450° oven.

FRUIT SNAPS

    1 ½ c. white sugar
    ½ c. brown sugar
    1 c. shortening
    3 eggs unbeaten
    ½ c. molasses
    3 ½ c. pastry flour
    1 tsp. baking soda
    ½ tsp. salt
    1 tsp. cinnamon
    1 tsp. cloves
    1 c. raisins & nuts

Mix. Drop onto greased baking sheet. Bake at 375 degrees.

CHOCOLATE CHIP COOKIES

    1 c. white sugar
    1 c. brown sugar
    1 tsp. baking soda in 2 Tbsp. hot water
    1 c. shortening
    ½ c. butter
    ½ c. Spry or Crisco
    3 egg yolks
    3 c. flour
    2 pkg sweet chocolate cut into small pieces.

Put chocolate in batter. Add 3 egg whites well beaten, 1 tsp. vanilla, 1 tsp. salt. Drop in pan. Bake at 375°.

COCAROONS

2 eggs whites
2 c. corn flakes
2 c. cocoanut
½ tsp. salt
¼ tsp. extract

Mix. Bake at 375°.

SUMBACKLES

1 c. brown sugar
1 c. white sugar
1 c. butter
1 c. lard
2 eggs
1 tsp. flavoring
Enough flour to form stiff dough.

Press into greased sumbackle pan. Bake at 375°.

POWDERED SUGAR COOKIES

1 c. butter (½ butter, ½ compound)
2/3 c. sugar
2 scant c. flour
½ c. nut meats
1 tsp. flavoring

Mix with hands. Pinch off dough in small balls. Press down with fork. Bake in 375 degree oven for 10 minutes.

Roll in powdered sugar.

CHOCOLATE COOKIE (INEZ ELLIS)

¼ c. shortening
1 egg
1 tsp. vanilla
¼ tsp. salt
2 sq. chocolate
1 c. light brown sugar
½ c. milk
1 ½ c. cake flour
½ tsp. baking soda
1 c. nut meats

Cream shortening, add sugar, well beaten eggs. Mix, add milk and vanilla, then flour sifted with salt and soda, add melted chocolate. Drop from spoon. Bake in moderate (350°) oven. Frost while a little warm with chocolate frosting.

CRISP SUGAR COOKIES

1 c. butter
2 c. sugar
2 tsp. vanilla
½ tsp. lemon extract
½ tsp. almond extract
2 tsp. nutmeg
½ tsp. salt
5 Tbsp. cream
3 eggs
3 ½ c. flour
2 tsp. cream of tartar

Cream butter and sugar, add nutmeg, flavoring, salt, cream and eggs. Beat 2 minutes. Add rest of ingredients, chill dough. Cut in thin slices. Place 3 inches apart on cookie sheet. Bake 12 minutes.

ROSETTES (*FOR AMY)

 2 eggs
 1 c. milk
 1 tsp. sugar
 ¼ tsp. salt
 1 c. flour (more if necessary)
 Lard for frying

Beat eggs, slightly, add milk and flour until about as thick as cream.

If rosettes drop from iron, grease and iron too hot, if soft, fried too fast, if blistered, eggs have been beaten too much.

PEANUT COOKIES

 ½ c. butter
 ½ c. sugar
 2 eggs
 1 tsp. baking powder
 3/4 c. chopped nuts
 1 c. flour

Drop in buttered tin, bake in moderate (350°) oven.

CHRISTMAS COOKIES (MRS. MARY MANNEY)

 3 lbs brown sugar
 2 grated nutmegs
 2 tsp. cloves
 2 tsp. cinnamon
 2 tsp. allspice
 ½ lb citron
 2 c. light molasses
 1 ½ c. warm water, 2 Tbsp. baking soda dissolved in it

ADD: 1 lb chopped nuts

6 well beaten eggs

7 or 8 c. flour

Let dough stand two or three days. Then cut in squares. Put more flour in roll stiff. Bake on greased cookie sheet.

MACAROONS (EASY)

2 egg whites beaten stiff

ADD: 1 scant c. sugar

3/4 c. cocoanut

2 c. Post Toasties or Corn Flakes

1 tsp. vanilla

No other moisture needed. Turn pan bottom up and grease. Drop from tsp. Bake at 375° until done.

PEANUT BUTTER COOKIES

½ c. brown sugar
½ c. white sugar
1 c. butter or shortening
½ c. peanut butter
1 egg
1 ½ c. flour
1 tsp. baking soda in flour
Pinch of salt

Drop from spoon onto greased cookie sheet, flatten with fork. Bake at 375° until done.

RAISIN JUMBLES

1 c. fat
2 c. sugar
2 eggs, beaten
2/3 c. thick sour cream
1 tsp. nutmeg
1 tsp. vanilla
½ tsp. lemon
4 c. flour
1 ½ tsp. baking soda
1 c. raisins

Cream fat and sugar. Mix well, add eggs and cream. Beat 2 min, add all other ingredients. Drop from spoon and bake on greased cookie sheet for 12 minutes in a moderate oven, 350°.

GINGER DROP COOKIES

    1 c. brown sugar
    3 ½ c. flour
    3/4 c. warm molasses
    2 tsp. baking soda
    1 tsp. cinnamon
    1 c. sour milk
    3/4 c. butter
    2 eggs
    2 tsp. ginger
    1 tsp. salt

Beat eggs, cream butter and sugar. Add well beaten eggs, add molasses and sour milk and flour sifted soda alternately to butter and sugar mixture. Drop from spoon and bake in moderate oven, 350°.

CORN FLAKE COOKIES

    7 c. corn flakes
    1 lb milk chocolate (sweet)
    2 sq. of bitter chocolate
    Add nut meats.

Melt chocolate. Add other ingredients while chocolate is warm. Drop onto greased cookie sheets and let cool.

KRISPIES MARSHMALLOW SQUARES

    1/3 c. butter
    ½ lb marshmallows (about 2 ½ dozen)
    ½ tsp. vanilla
    1 pkg Kellogg's Rice Krispies

Melt butter and marshmallows in double boiler. Add vanilla, beat thoroughly. Put Krispies in large, buttered bowl and pour in marshmallow mixture. Stir briskly, press into shallow pan. When cool, cut in squares.

FRUIT COOKIES

3 eggs

1 c. white sugar

½ c. brown sugar

1 c. lard

2 c. molasses

1 c. sour milk

1 tsp. baking soda

Cinnamon, cloves, vanilla, grind raisins and nuts, flour to roll. Roll out, cut out cookies, place on greased baking sheet. Bake at 375° until done.

MACAROONS

1 c. butter

1 c. white sugar

2 eggs

1 tsp. vanilla

2 c. flour

1 tsp. baking soda

1 tsp. baking powder

1 tsp. salt

2 c. oatmeal

1 c. cocoanut

Nutmeats

Roll into balls, put quite far apart to bake. Bake at 350 degree for 10 to 12 minutes.

DATE BALLS

2/3 c. fat

2 eggs

2 tsp. cinnamon

½ tsp. nutmeg

1 tsp. vanilla

4 c. flour

1 ½ c. brown sugar

3 Tbsp. cream

1 tsp. cloves

¼ tsp. salt

1 c. chopped dates

1 tsp. baking soda

Cream fat and sugar.

Add eggs & cream, beat well. Add rest of ingredients and drop small portions from tip of spoon onto greased baking sheets. Space 3 inches apart. Bake 12 minutes at 375 degrees.

HONEY COOKIES

2 c. honey

1 c. lard

Rind of 1 orange

½ c. hot water

4 level tsp. baking soda

1 c. sugar

4 eggs

Rind of 1 lemon

1 tsp. salt

8 c. sifted flour

Roll and cut. Place on greased cookie sheet. Bake in moderate oven, 350°.

HERMITS

2 c. light brown sugar

2/3 c. butter

3 eggs

½ c. sweet milk

1 tsp. baking soda

1 tsp. baking powder

1 tsp. cinnamon

1 tsp. cloves

1 tsp. nutmeg

1 tsp. ginger

1 tsp. allspice

4 c. flour

1/8 tsp. salt

1 c. chopped raisins

Cream butter and sugar. Add well beaten eggs with milk. Sift flour, spices, salt, soda, baking powder together. Add to mixture. Add raisins. Drop on greased and floured cookie sheet. Bake 12 minutes in hot oven (450°).

DROP NUT COOKIES

1 ½ c. light brown sugar
½ c. butter
2 eggs
3 Tbsp. cream
1 tsp. vanilla
½ tsp. salt
1 c. finely chopped nuts
2 2/3 c. flour
2 tsp. baking powder

Cream butter and sugar. Beat eggs, add cream, then nuts and vanilla, salt and baking powder with flour. Drop from tsp, bake 15 minutes in hot oven, 450°.

RAISIN HONEY GEMS (HELEN MANNEY) (VERY GOOD!)

Makes 80 to 100 Cookies, very good

1 ½ c. honey
1 egg
½ tsp. salt
2 ¼ tsp. baking powder
1 tsp. cinnamon
1 ½ c. oatmeal (uncooked)
1 c. raisins
2 Tbsp. hot water
3/4 c. shortening
2 ½ c. flour
¼ tsp. baking soda

Can add dates and nutmeats. Pour hot water over dates after they are cut fine. Cream honey and shortening, add egg. Sift flour, salt, soda, baking powder, & cinnamon into mixture.

Add oatmeal, raisins, nuts and dates with water. Mix thoroughly. Drop by tsp. onto greased cookie sheet. Bake in 375 degree oven for 15 to 20 minutes. Pat dough down with tsp.

SPRITZ BAKKELS

Make dough of 1 scant c. sugar; 1 c. butter or shortening; 3 Tbsp. thick cream; flour enough for thin dough to press thru cookie press. Bake at 375° until done.

Can be decorated anyway you like.

Sand Bakkels (Mrs. Akerhaugen)

    1 c. brown sugar
    1 c. shortening (some butter)
    1 egg
    2 ½ c. flour, sifted
    pinch of salt

Mix. Press into fluted molds. Bake at 375° until done.

Sand Bakkels

    1 c. sugar (scant)
    1 c. shortening (some butter)
    ¼ tsp. salt
    3 c. flour (sift & then measure)
    3 egg yolks
    2 Tbsp. thick cream

Mix. Press into fluted molds. Bake at 375° until done.

Oatmeal Squares

Rub together:

    2 ½ c. oatmeal
    1 c. shortening
    2 c. flour
    1 c. brown sugar
    ½ tsp. salt

Over that mixture pour:

    1 Tbsp. boiling water with -
    ½ tsp. baking soda

FILLING:

1 small package dates

1 c. sugar

1 c. water

Boil filling ingredients until thick. Let cool. Layer of first mixture on cookie sheet, then layer of date filling, then layer of first mixture on top. Bake ½ hour in 350 degree oven. Cut in squares.

RAISIN MOLASSES COOKIES

¾ c. shortening

1 c. sugar

1 egg

1 c. light molasses

4 ½ c. flour

¼ tsp. cinnamon

¼ tsp. ginger

1 ½ tsp. baking soda

¾ c. boiling water

1 c. seedless raisins

Cream shortening with sugar, add unbeaten egg, molasses, and mix thoroughly. Add alternately the flour sifted with spices and the boiling water. Add soda to last portions of water. Add raisins and beat thoroughly. Drop by spoonfuls onto greased pan and bake 10 minutes in a hot, 400° oven.

OLSON'S COOKIES

GRIND together:

1 c. raisins

½ c. cocoanut

THEN:

2 eggs

2 c. brown sugar

2 c. oatmeal (quick)

1 c. shortening

1 tsp. baking soda dissolved in 2 Tbsp. hot water

2 c. flour (sifted)

2 tsp. vanilla

1 c. corn flakes

Nuts

Grease cookie sheet, spread thin with fork. Bake 375 degree oven.

Mrs. Akerhaugen's Oatmeal Refrigerator Cookies

1 c. shortening

1 c. white sugar

1 c. brown sugar

2 eggs

½ c. flour

1 tsp. baking soda

1 tsp. Salt

3 c. Quick Oatmeal

1 tsp. vanilla

Mix. Drop onto greased baking sheet. Bake at 375° until done.

MOLASSES COOKIES (DOROTHY RUSSELL)

    3/4 c. shortening
    1 c. brown sugar
    1 egg
    3 Tbsp. molasses
    ¼ tsp. salt
    2 ¼ c. flour
    2 tsp. baking soda
    ¼ tsp. cloves
    ½ tsp. cinnamon
    1 tsp. ginger (scant)

Shape dough in balls the size of a walnut. Put on greased cookie sheet. Flatten with a fork. Sprinkle tops with sugar. Bake in 375 degree oven.

OLSON'S (GOOD)

SIFT together:

    1 1/3 c. sifted flour
    ½ tsp. baking powder

BLEND together:

    1/3 c. butter or oleo
    ½ c. firmly packed brown sugar

Add dry ingredients, mix with mixer until like coarse meal.

Stir in ¼ c. pecans, chopped. Mix well. Pack into well greased pan 12x8x2 or 13x9. Bake in 350 degree oven for 10 minutes only, remove from oven, put on topping.

TOPPING:
Beat 2 eggs until foamy, add 3/4 c. dark corn syrup, ¼ c. packed brown sugar, 3 Tbsp. flour; 1 tsp. salt, 1 tsp. vanilla.

Mix well, pour over cookies that have baked for 10 minutes. Sprinkle with 3/4 c. shopped pecans. Bake 350 degree oven for 25 to 30 minutes. Let cool. Cut into bars.

MINNIE'S COOKIE

1 c. butter
½ c. powdered sugar
2 c. flour
½ c. pecans cut fine
1 tsp. vanilla

Bake in 350 degree oven for 12 to 15 minutes, not too brown, they burn easily. While still hot, roll in powdered sugar, then roll in powdered sugar again when cool.

CHOCOLATE COOKIES

1 c. brown sugar
½ c. butter
Pinch of salt
2 eggs
1 ½ c. flour
2 sq of chocolate, melted
½ c. sweet milk
½ tsp. baking soda in milk
1 c. nut meats
1 c. raisins
1 tsp. vanilla

Drop onto greased baking sheet. Bake at 375° until done. Frost cookies when cool.

DESSERTS

LEMON PUDDING

Make in the order given:

> 1 c. sugar
> 3 Tbsp. flour (level)
> 1 c. sweet milk
> Yolks of 2 eggs
> Juice of 1 lemon & the lemon's grated rind
> Beaten whites of 2 eggs (beaten stiff)

Fold in the beaten egg whites into the other ingredients. Add a pinch of salt. Pour into a buttered casserole dish set in a pan of water. Bake at 325°. When done, crust will be lightly browned.

May be served warm or cold; with or without whipped cream. There is a lemon pudding bottom and light cake-like crust on top when done.

BUTTER SCOTCH PUDDING

> 1 c. dark brown sugar
> 1/3 c. flour
> 1 tsp. salt
> 2 eggs
> 2 c. milk
> 1 tsp. vanilla
> 2 Tbsp. butter

Blend sugar, flour, salt and add eggs & milk. Cook in double boiler until thick, stirring frequently. Pour in glass dishes and chill. Serve plain or with whipped cream.

STEAMED CHERRY PUDDING

    3 Tbsp. fat (e.g. Crisco)
    1 c. sugar
    2 eggs
    1 c. milk
    ½ tsp. salt
    1 tsp. vanilla
    1 tsp. cinnamon
    3 c. flour
    3 tsp. Baking Powder
    3 c. cherries

Cream fat and sugar. Add rest of ingredients and beat 2 minutes. Pour into buttered mold. Cover tightly and steam 3 hours.

Serve warm.

CHERRY SAUCE

    1 c. sugar
    2 Tbsp. flour
    1/8 tsp. salt
    1 ½ c. water
    2 Tbsp. lemon juice
    1 c. seeded cherries
    1 Tbsp. butter

Blend sugar and flour. Add rest of ingredients. Boil gently on stove, stirring constantly until thick.

Serve warm.

MAPLE WALNUT CREAM PUDDING

    2 c. milk
    1 c. maple syrup
    2 Tbsp. cornstarch
    1 c. cream
    ¼ tsp. salt
    2 eggs
    1 c. chopped nuts

Heat 1 ¾ c. milk in double boiler with 1 c. syrup. Mix rest of milk with cornstarch and salt. Stir into mixture. Cook, add beaten egg, cook a few more minutes. Then add nuts.

Serve with whipped cream.

DELICATE PUDDING

    1 ½ c. water
    ½ c. sugar
    ½ tsp. salt

Mix well and bring to boiling point. Mix 3 Tbsp. cornstarch in water. Stir into boiling syrup & cook until thick. Beat whites of 3 eggs. Whip the hot mixture into them, return to fire for 1 minute to set the egg. Add ½ c. lemon juice and a little grated lemon rind.

Turn at once into mold that has been wet with cold water.

Put in ice box (refrigerator) to chill.

Serve with a custard sauce, strawberries or any fruit, or whipped cream sprinkled with colored sugar.

CARROT PUDDING

½ c. fat (e.g. Crisco)
2 Tbsp. molasses
1 c. grated raw carrots
1 tsp. cinnamon
½ tsp. cloves
½ c. currants
2 Tbsp. chopped lemon peel
2 Tbsp. hot water
1 tsp. baking soda
1 c. sugar
1 egg
½ tsp. nutmeg
½ tsp. salt
½ c. raisins
2 c. flour
1 tsp. baking powder

Cream fat and sugar. Add rest of ingredients and half fill buttered mold. Cover tightly. Steam 2 hours.

Serve with warm lemon sauce (below).

LEMON SAUCE

1 c. sugar
2 Tbsp. flour
1/3 c. lemon juice
1 tsp. grated lemon rind
2 Tbsp. butter
1 2/3 c. water

Blend sugar & flour. Add lemon juice, rind, and water. Boil 1 min. Add butter and mix. Serve warm.

RICE KRISPIES DATE PUDDING

2 eggs
1 c. sugar
4 tsp. sweet milk
1 tsp. baking powder
1 c. Rice Krispies crumbs
1 c. chopped nut meats
1 c. chopped dates

Beat eggs. Add sugar and milk. Mis baking powder with crumbs. Add to first mixture, along with nuts and dates. Put into buttered baking dish and set in a pan of hot water. Bake at 375° for 40 min.

Serve plain or with whipped cream.

8 servings.

DATE PUDDING

1 c. sugar
2 Tbsp. flour
1 tsp. baking powder
¼ tsp. salt

Mix dry ingredients. Add 2, well-beaten, eggs. Beat all until light.

Add 1 c. chopped dates, 1 c. chopped walnut meats.

Bake 30 min in 350° oven.

Serve either plain or with whipped cream.

CORN FLAKE STRUDEL

Line a pudding dish with corn flakes, crushed and buttered. Cover with thinly sliced apples. Sprinkle with sugar mixed with a little cinnamon. Sprinkle with pieces of butter. Fill to top with alternating layers. Final layer should be a layer of Corn Flakes.

Cover dish closely. Bake in moderate 350° oven until apples are soft.

Serve with lemon sauce or whipped cream.

LEMON BIOQUE

    1 c. (13 oz can milk or 2 c. (½ pt) cream)
    1 package lemon Jell-O or gelatin
    1 1/3 c. water
    1/3 c. honey
    1/8 tsp. salt
    3 Tbsp. lemon juice
    Grated lemon rind from 1 lemon
    2 ½ c. vanilla wafers, crumbled

Thoroughly chill milk/cream overnight. Dissolve Jell-O or gelatin in water. Add honey, salt & lemon or orange juice & rind. Set in refrigerator.

When set, beat in milk (or cream) that has been whipped stiff. Whip gelatin mixture.

Place crumbs in a well-buttered cake pan.

Pour in mixture & put some crumbs on top.

Place in refrigerator.

Make the night before needed.

CHERRY DELIGHT

Grease sides and bottom of oblong pan 13 x 9 ½ ".

> 1 no. 2 can pitted sour cherries, including juice
> ½ c. sugar
> ¼ tsp. red food coloring

Mix above in oblong pan.

Mix white cake mix. Fold in ½ c. chopped nuts. Pour batter over cherries. Bake 45 – 50 min in 350° oven. Cool slightly. Invert on large serving plate. Serve warm, plain or with whipped cream.

BRIDAL PUDDING

> 1 envelope Knox gelatin dissolved in ½ c. boiling water, let cool.
> Whip 1 pint of cream

Fold 6 beaten egg whites into whipped cream. Add to gelatin mixture. Add ¾ c. powdered sugar and a pinch of salt. Add 1 tsp. vanilla. Let set partially and pour into a pan with the bottom covered with chocolate cookies crumbled.

Save some of the crumbs for the top.

Let stand in refrigerator three or four hours.

STRAWBERRY ANGEL LOAF

1 3oz package strawberry Jell-O
1 c. hot water
1/3 c. sugar
2 c. heavy cream, whipped
2 c. crushed sweetened fresh or frozen strawberries
1 loaf angel food cake

Dissolve gelatin in hot water. Chill until partially set. Fold sugar into cream, fold in strawberries and fold mixture into partially-set gelatin.

Cut cake crosswise into 3 layers. Fill layers and frost cake with strawberry mixture. Chill until firm (about 1 ½ hours). Garnish with fresh strawberries.

CARAMELLED PEACHES

1 8oz package cream cheese
¼ c. light cream
A few drops of almond extract
½ c. walnuts, chopped
2 1lb cans (4 c.) peach halves, chilled & drained
1 recipe caramel candy sauce

Soften cream cheese. Add cream and beat until fluffy. Add almond extract and nuts. Mix well. Fill peach halves generously with cream cheese mixture. Place two peach halves together to form a whole peach. Press gently so cheese fluffs out around edges.

Serve with caramel candy sauce made from ½ lb caramels, 1/3 c. water. Put caramels and water in double boiler and stir constantly until melted and smooth. Makes 2/3 c.

FRUIT FILLED CRESCENTS

¼ c. lemon juice, fresh or frozen
1 ½ c. heavy whipping cream, whipped
½ c. sifted confectioners sugar
1 lb can (2 c.) fruit cocktail, chilled & drained
1/3 c. chopped walnuts
6 sponge cake dessert cups

Stir lemon juice into whipped cream, fold in sugar. Combine 1/3 of cream mixture with fruit cocktail and nuts. Spoon into dessert cup.

Invert 1 dessert cup over another so fruit mixture is in the center.

Frost with the remaining whipped cream mixture. Cut each stack in half. Garnish with ½ walnut. Serve with additional fruit cocktail.

GRAHAM CRACKER DESSERT

1 lb graham crackers
1 c. chopped dates
1 c. broken nut meats
1 c. diced marshmallows
½ c. cream
1/3 tsp. salt

Roll crackers and add rest of ingredients. Pack into a mold, chill for several hours. Slice and serve with whipped cream.

ORANGE DELIGHT

    3 c. sliced oranges
    ½ c. sugar
    2 Tbsp. lemon juice
    ½ c. cocoanut

Mix oranges, sugar, lemon juice and marshmallows. Pour into glass dish. Sprinkle with cocoanut. Chill 1 hour or longer. Serve in glasses.

PINEAPPLE DESSERT

    ½ lb marshmallows
    1 can crush pineapple

Melt marshmallows in double boiler. When marshmallows are melted and cool, add ½ pint whipped cream. Have crust in pie tin made of 18 crushed graham crackers, ½ c. melted butter, ½ c. brown sugar, and reserve a few crumbs to put on top.

Serve with whipped cream.

Make the day before.

CHOCOLATE DESSERT

    ½ c. sweet milk
    30 marshmallows

Melt marshmallows in double boiler. Beat with rotary egg beater. Let cool.

Beat 1 c. cream, add 1 Tbsp. sugar and a pinch of salt. Fold into above mixture 2 squares of chocolate, grated. Take 18 graham crackers (or more) roll, add 1/3 c. melted butter, pat crumbs into pie tin bottom and sides. Save some crumbs for the top.

Bake crust a few minutes. Add above mixture. Pat crumbs on top. Let cool/stand for 2 hours.

APPLE BROWN BETTY

    1 c. soft bread crumbs
    1 ½ c. sliced apples
    ½ c. sugar
    ½ tsp. cinnamon
    1/8 tsp. salt
    ½ tsp. vanilla
    4 Tbsp. butter, melted
    2/3 c. water

Mix all together, pour into buttered baking dish. Cover & bake for 30 min in a moderate 350° oven.

SAUCE FOR APPLE BROWN BETTY

    3 Tbsp. Butter
    2 Tbsp. hot cream
    1/14 tsp. vanilla
    ¼ tsp. lemon
    1/8 tsp. salt
    1 tsp. sifted confectionary sugar

Mix and server on top of pudding.

Marshmallow Roll

½ lb graham crackers
½ lb marshmallows
½ c. nut meats
½ package of dates
1 c. crushed pineapple, drained
1 c. cream

Roll graham crackers and save three for the outside of the roll. Cut dates, marshmallows in flour into fine pieces. Chop nuts. Mix all together. Add cream and mix into a roll. Crush three graham crackers and roll around. Wrap in wax paper. Put in a cool place until set.

Apple Dessert (Adah Shimer)

½ c. flour
¾ c. white sugar
1 tsp. baking powder
Sift those three together.
Add a pinch of salt.
Add well-beaten egg
¼ c. chopped nut meats
1 tsp. vanilla
2 apples, peeled and diced

Mix. Bake 25 minutes in 350° oven. Serve with or without whipped cream.

ANGEL FOOD ICE BOX DESSERT

1 large Angel Food Cake
Make a custard from the following:
Boil 1 c. sugar
1 pint milk
Pinch of salt
Yolks of 2 eggs, beaten
1 tsp. vanilla
2 Tbsp. gelatin soaked in cold water for ten minutes. Let cool and set

Add 2 beaten egg whites to 1 pint of whipped cream. Add nuts, cherries or pineapple, shredded.

Break angel food into small pieces. Put layer in large pan, alternatingly with above custard over it. Place a final layer of cake on top. Let stand in ice box overnight. Cut into squares to serve, topped with whipped cream and a cherry.

DELICATE BANANA BETTY

4 bananas
1 ½ c. Rice Krispies
¾ c. brown sugar
¼ c. butter
Orange or lemon juice
½ c. Rice Krispies

Alternate layer of bananas sprinkled with crushed Rice Krispies. On top of banana layer, sprinkle brown sugar. Dot with butter & orange juice. Sprinkle ½ c. Rice Krispies over top. Add enough milk to half fill pudding dish. Cover and bake 20-30 minutes at 350°. Uncover last 5 minutes to brown. Serve hot.

BAKED BANANAS

Dip bananas in lemon juice. Then roll in corn flakes mixed with brown sugar. Bake at 350° for 30 minutes.

CORN FLAKE CHARLOTTE

    2 ½ c. Corn Flakes
    2 c. sweetened apple sauce
    Rind of ½ lemon or orange and juice of ½ orange or lemon
    2 Tbsp. butter

Spread layer of corn flake crumbs. Cover with apple sauce to which fruit juice has been added. Top with corn flakes. Dot with butter.

Bake 15 minutes in 400° oven. Serve with whipped cream.

HONEY KRISP ROLL

    1 c. Rice Krispies, crushed/rolled (measure after crushing)
    ½ c. chopped dates
    ¼ c. chopped nut meats
    8 marshmallows, cut into pieces
    ½ pint whipping cream
    ½ c. rolled Rice Krispies for outside of roll.

Mix all ingredients except whipping cream and ½ c. Rice Krispies.

Whip cream. Fold into mixture. Shape in roll and roll in ½ c. Rice Krispies. Put in mold lined with waxed paper. Chill 4-6 hours.

Will keep several days. Slice served with whipped cream and cherry on top.

CHOCOLATE DESSERT

    4 egg yolks
    2/3 c. milk
    3 Tbsp. sugar
    Cook in double boiler until thick
    Soften 1 package of gelatin in 3 Tbsp. water. Fix this while first
    mixture is cooking.
    Add chopped nuts & cut up candy bar.
    Cool.
    Beat 4 egg whites until stiff.
    Add 2 Tbsp. sugar & beat
    Add to custard.

Can be served with or without whipped cream.

STRAWBERRY DESSERT (BETTY)

    Crush soda crackers
    Spread with beaten egg whites & sugar
    Bake slightly.
    Then cover with fresh frozen strawberries.
    Top with whipped cream.

BRIDAL PUDDING

    1 envelope Knox gelatin dissolved in ½ c. cold water
    Add ½ c. boiling water & let cool.
    Whip 1 pt. cream & fold in 6 beaten egg whites
    Add to gelatin mixture.
    Add ¾ c. powdered sugar
    Pinch of salt
    1 tsp. vanilla

Let partially set & pour in pan with bottom covered with chocolate cookie
crumbs.

Save some cookie crumbs for the top.

Let stand in refrigerator 3-4 hours.

FROZEN PRUNE WHIP

¾ c. cooked prune pulp (baby food)

2 eggs

½ c. confectioner's sugar

½ c. orange juice

¼ tsp. salt

1 c. whipping cream

Beat eggs and add sugar gradually. Add prune pulp, orange juice & salt. Mix well. Fold in whipped cream. Pour into tray and freeze.

NABISCO DESSERT

1 lb Apricots, cooked, or 2 boxes strawberries (can be frozen)

1 ½ lb Nabiscoes (Graham Crackers)

1 c. butter

2 c. powdered sugar

3 egg yolks, beaten well

1 pint whipping cream.

Roll Nabiscoes until fine crumbs. Put into buttered pan. Mix all ingredients except crushed Nabiscoes. Beat 3 egg whites. Fold into mixture. Put layers of Nabiscoes, fruit whipping cream. Finish with Nabiscoes on top.

QUICK RASPBERRY PARFAIT

1 package vanilla pudding

2 each 12 oz. package frozen raspberries, thawed, or 1 pint fresh sweetened berries

Instant whipped cream topping or whipped cream

Prepare pudding according to the directions. When pudding is thick, alternate layers of pudding & raspberries in sherbet glasses. Top with whipped cream.

CHOCOLATE SAUCE

1 6oz. package semi-sweet chocolate

¾ c. light corn syrup, poured over chocolate

Heat but not boil

Add:

1/3 c. milk

2 Tbsp. butter

1 tsp. vanilla.

If too thick, add 2 Tbsp. milk, cream or water.

MRS. BOWLES' DESSERT

3 egg whites, beaten stiff

1 pint whipping cream, whipped

Fold together

½ c. sugar

Small bottle of maraschino cherries, cut

1 small can crushed pineapple, drained

¾ c. chopped nut meats

Mix together and freeze in a loaf pan.

CHERRY CHEESE TARTS

    3/4 c. sugar
    2 ea. 8 oz. packages cream cheese
    3 beaten eggs
    1 tsp. vanilla
    1 pkg. vanilla wafers
    Cherry Pie filling

Put one vanilla wafer in bottom of each of 24 medium aluminum foil muffin cups.

Beat sugar and cream cheese until well blended. Add eggs and vanilla - mix well. Spoon over wafers.

Bake at 350 degrees for 15 minutes until set. Let stand 5 minutes until center drops a little. Top with a teaspoon of pie filling.

Frosting

Cream Lemon Frosting

CREAM TOGETHER:

>   ¼ c. Spry shortening
>   1 ea 3 oz. package cream cheese
>   3 ½ c. powdered sugar

ADD:

>   ½ c. sugar
>   Dash of salt
>   2 Tbsp. lemon juice
>   Grated rind of lemon

Blend thoroughly. Add remaining ½ of sugar with 2 Tbsp. of milk or cream. If not enough cream, add enough so you can spread it. Add a few drops of yellow coloring.

Chocolate Frosting

>   2 c. powdered sugar
>   2 Tbsp. cream
>   3 or 4 marshmallows
>   1 ½ sq. chocolate, cut fine
>   4 Tbsp. butter

Mix last four ingredients. Then gradually add the powdered sugar and 1 tsp. of your favorite flavoring.

CUSTARD SAUCE FOR ANGEL FOOD CAKE

    5 egg yolks
    1/3 c. sugar
    1 c. cream

Mix. Heat in a double boiler until thick. Can add nuts, vanilla, grated rind and juice of 1 lemon, if desire.

SPICY FROSTING

    3 Tbsp. hot coffee
    1 tsp. vanilla
    2 Tbsp. butter
    1/8 tsp. salt
    1 1/3 c. sifted powdered sugar

Mix ingredients. Beat for 3 minutes until thick. Frost top of cake.

SMALL SEVEN MINUTE FROSTING

    3 Tbsp. water
    1 egg white
    1/8 tsp. cream of tartar
    2 tsp. corn syrup
    ¾ c. sugar

Mix and beat in a double boiler (simmering) for 7 minutes or until stiff.

Remove from heat and add ½ tsp. vanilla.

FRENCH PASTRY FROSTING

> 1 Tbsp. butter
> 1 Tbsp. hot cream
> 1 tsp. vanilla
> 1 ¼ c. confectioner's sugar

Mix ingredients and beat until creamy.

JELLY FROSTING

> Combine in a double boiler:
> ½ c. tart jelly
> 1 unbeaten egg white

Heat over hot water until fluffy.

BOILED HONEY FROSTING

> 1 ½ c. honey
> 1/8 tsp. salt
> 1 egg white
> 1 tsp. vanilla

Cook honey & salt until it threads.

Beat egg white. Pour syrup slowly into beaten egg white. Beat until it stands in peaks. Add vanilla.

Spread over cake.

You can add chopped fruits and nuts, if desired.

SAUCE FOR ANGEL FOOD

1 c. sugar
5 Tbsp. cake flour
½ c. whipping cream
4 Tbsp. water
3 Tbsp. lemon juice
½ Tbsp. orange juice
Rind of orange, grated
1 beaten egg
2 Tbsp. butter

Combine sugar, flour and add juice and water. Add beaten egg. Cook until thick.

Remove from heat. Add butter, rind and whipping cream.

CREAM CHEESE FROSTING

1 Tbsp. milk
1 3-oz package of cream cheese (6 Tbsp)
Gradually blend in 2 ½ c. sifted confectioners' sugar
Add 1 square unsweetened chocolate, melted and slightly cooled
1 tsp. vanilla
1 tsp. salt

Mix and frost cake.

HILDA'S FROSTING

½ c. brown sugar, packed
6 Tbsp. butter
Melt those slowly.
Then add:
1/3 c. milk

Boil for 2 minutes after it starts to boil.

Let mixture cool

Then add: 1 ½ c. powdered sugar, ¼ tsp. salt, 1 tsp. vanilla.

Beat until spreading consistency.

SAUCE FOR ANGEL FOOD (CRANBERRY)

> 1 c. cranberries, ground
> 1 c. apples, diced
> ¼ c. drained pineapple tidbits
> 1 c. sugar
> 1/8 tsp. salt

Mix and let stand overnight. Before serving, add ½ pint of thickly whipped cream.

ROSE LAZY DAISY FROSTING

> ¾ c. brown sugar
> ½ c. melted butter
> ¼ c. cream
> 1 c. cocoanut

Combine all ingredients. Blend well. When cake is done, frost and return cake to oven under the broiler and brown.

FRESH BERRY TOPPING (FOR SPONGE OR ANGEL FOOD CAKE)

> 1 egg white
> Dash of salt
> ½ c. crushed berries
> 1 ½ c. sifted powdered sugar

Beat egg white and salt until frothy. Add berries. Then add sugar gradually. Beat until thick and fluffy.

Rich Lemon Filling

4 Tbsp. cake flour
¾ c. sugar
Dash of salt
¼ c. lemon juice
2 Tbsp. butter
½ c. water
1 egg, well beaten
½ tsp. grated lemon rind

Combine flour, sugar and salt in top of double boiler. Add lemon juice, water & egg. Cook over boiling water for 10 minutes or until thickened, stirring constantly.

Add butter & lemon rind.

Cool.

Easter Bonnet Frosting

2 egg whites
1 each 1 lb jar of strawberry preserves
1 tsp. lemon juice
¼ tsp. grated lemon rind

Beat egg whites until stiff. Heat 1 c. strawberry preserves over low heat until bubbly. Add lemon juice & rind. Pour preserves slowly into egg whites, beating constantly until mixture stands in peaks.

Bake two layer cake and put 1/3 c. plain strawberry preserves between the layers. Then this frosting on top. Also frost cake sides with remaining frosting.

LEMON FROSTING
Frosts 2 ea 9" layers or one 13" x 9 ½" loaf cake

    2 ¾ c. powdered sugar (sift if lumpy)

    ½ tsp. salt

    1 egg

    1 Tbsp. light corn syrup

    ½ c. shortening

    1 tsp. vanilla

    1 Tbsp. lemon juice

    1 Tbsp. grated lemon peel

Mix sugar, salt & egg. Blend in syrup. Add shortening, vanilla, lemon juice & peel. Mix until smooth & creamy. Add more sugar to thicken or water to thin until of spreading consistency.

ORANGE FROSTING (LARRY'S BIRTHDAY CAKE)

    1/3 c. shortening

    3 ½ c. confectioner's sugar (sift if lumpy)

    2 Tbsp. corn syrup

    ¼ tsp. salt

    1 Tbsp. grated orange peel

    ¼ c. orange juice

Combine shortening, corn syrup, salt, 1 c. sugar & orange peel. Add remaining sugar & orange juice alternately, mixing until smooth and creamy.

Add more sugar to thicken or juice to think frosting, if required until of spreading consistency.

Hot Dishes & Beans

Frankfurter Corn Bake

    3 eggs, slightly beaten
    2 cans (17 oz) cream style corn
    1 c. fine bread crumbs
    ¼ c. chopped onion
    1 tsp. dry mustard
    1 tsp. salt
    8-6 frankfurters, cut fine, ½ in slices

Beat eggs slightly in large bowl, add remaining ingredients, save enough frankfurters for garnish on top. Bake in well-greased pan (shallow), 1 ½ to 2 qt. size. Arrange few frankfurters on top for garnish. Bake 375° oven for 30 minutes. Can garnish with catsup in center.

Hot Dish - Hamburger

    Layer Sliced Raw Potatoes
    Layer hamburger, fried with onions
    Layer green peas

Pour over tomatoes, sprinkle with salt and pepper. Put crumbs on top. Bake 375° oven for 30 minutes or until heated thoroughly.

HOT DISH - LAYERED

    Layer rice (cook 2 cups)
    Layer tomatoes (1 can)
    Layer meat fried with onions
    Layer peas (1 can)
    Layer rice

Cover with crumbs. Bake 375° oven for 30 minutes or until heated thoroughly.

HOT DISH — SALMON

    Layer of noodles (package cooked, small)
    Layer of salmon, 1 can
    Layer of celery, 1 stalk
    Layer of peas, 1 can
    Layer of noodles

Pour white sauce over. Bake 375° oven for 30 minutes or until heated thoroughly.

CHILE CON CARNE

35 cents round steak, browned in butter. Then cover with water and boil until done. Add salt, onions, 1 can tomatoes, ½ package spaghetti or macaroni (cooked), add to rest of dish. Then add tomatoes, cook ½ hour at 350°.

Author's note: get a pound of round steak. I doubt 35¢ will get you any stead, round or otherwise, anymore.

KRAFT MACARONI CHEESE DINNER

    1 Package Kraft Macaroni & Cheese Dinner

    1 can peas

    1 can tuna fish

    1 can pimento

    1 can celery soup

Put all together and bake ½ hour in casserole at 350°.

SPANISH RICE

    1 c. cooked rice

    1 Onion

    1 Tbsp. fat

    1 pt. tomatoes

    Salt & Pepper

Heat fat or two slices of bacon. Add rice, chopped onion and cook until brown. Put in greased baking dish. Pour over tomatoes, juice and pulp. Cook until brown. Bake 30 minutes in a moderate oven, 350°.

CREAMED CHICKEN WITH PEAS

    3 Tbsp. butter

    1 ¼ c. milk

    3 Tbsp. flour

    1 c. cooked chicken

    Salt & Pepper

Put butter in pan and blend in flour. Gradually stir in milk. Season to taste and add chicken and peas. Simmer for 10 minutes. Serve with rolls or toast.

HOT DISH (MYRTLE)

1 ½ lbs ground round steak
2 small onions, chopped
2 c. celery cut fine
1 can chicken soup with rice
1 can mushrooms
2 tsp. chow mein sauce
2 tsp. Worcestershire sauce
½ c. raw rice, cooked
2 c. water
Salt & Pepper

Bake 2 hours at 350°, cover with chow mein noodles, finish baking.

TUNA VEGETABLE PIE

DICE & simmer for 15 minutes:

1 c. water
½ tsp. salt
½ c. raw carrot
1 c. raw potato
3 Tbsp. chopped onion

ADD & simmer for 5 minutes:

1 c. green peas, canned or frozen

Drain, saving liquids. Melt 2 Tbsp. butter in a saucepan, add oil from 1 can flaked tuna, stir in 2 Tbsp. flour.

ADD: 2 c. liquid from vegetables plus milk, ½ tsp. salt, & a dash of pepper.

COOK: until thickened, stirring constantly.

ADD: vegetables and 1 7 oz. can tuna.

BAKE: 25 to 30 min. with pastry topping of:

> 1 c. flour
> ½ tsp. salt
> 1/3 c. shortening
> 2 Tbsp. water

Roll out and put on top of hot dish.

HOT DISH – HAM

> Layer of raw potatoes
> Layer of pieces of ham
> 1 can tomato soup

Bake 1 hour at 350°.

HOT DISH – HAMBURGER

> 1 pkg of egg noodles
> 1 can mushrooms
> 1 jar pimentos
> 1 lb hamburger

And a little chopped:

> Green pepper
> Celery
> Onion

Make a cream sauce and mix all together, first boiling noodles, onions, celery, and peppers. Add other ingredients. Fry hamburger. Put in greased casserole and bake 375° oven for 30 minutes or until heated thoroughly.

HOT DISH (MRS. HERRICK)

1 lb hamburger

1 can whole kernel corn

1 green pepper

2 small onions

1 stalk celery

1 can tomato soup

1 egg

Salt & Pepper

1 c. boiled rice

Brown meat, onion, & celery. Combine mixture. Bake for 1 hour at 350°.

HOT DISH (MRS. NELSON)

1 pkg noodles

1 can kernel corn

2 cans tomato soup

½ lb bacon, cut fine

1 onion, chopped fine

1 Green pepper, chopped fine

Chili powder (to taste)

Salt & pepper (to taste)

Little sugar

Cook noodles, fry bacon, onion & green pepper. Add corn and seasoning (chili powder) to noodles and tomato soup. Bake at 350° for 45 min (or until heated through), remove from oven and put crushed corn flakes on top, let brown for a few minutes.

AMERICAN CHOP SUEY

    1 pkg noodles
    3/4 lb chopped veal
    3/4 lb chopped pork
    1 can corn
    1 green pepper, chopped
    1 celery stalk, chopped
    1 can chicken soup

Cook meat and salt, add cooked noodles to meat. Add remaining ingredients, cover with bread crumbs and bake for 3/4 hour.

VEAL FIESTAS

    1 ½ lbs veal steak
    Salt & Pepper
    ¼ c. flour
    5 Tbsp. shortening
    ½ c. chili sauce
    1 ½ c. hot water
    ½ c. grated cheese
    1 ½ c. cooked macaroni
    3 large onions, sliced

Cut veal into serving size pieces. Season well and dredge with flour. Brown both sides in hot fat, cover with sliced onions, chili sauce and hot water. Cover skilled and cook slowly for 30 minutes. Remove cover, sprinkle with cheese, cook 10 minutes until cheese melts. Remove meat to platter, stir cooked macaroni into gravy in pan and heat. Pour around meat on platter.

HOT DISH — ROUND STEAK

2 c. cooked rice
2 lbs round steak, fried
2 lbs veal, fried
1 can peas
1 can tomatoes
1 can tomato juice
2 onions
2 c. celery, boiled

Combine and place in greased casserole. Bake 1 hour at 350°.

CHILI CON CARNE

½ lbs beef, diced
1 c. cooked kidney beans
3 tsp. bacon fat
1 tsp. chopped celery
1 Tbsp. chopped onion
¼ tsp. chili powder
¼ tsp. paprika
½ c. water
¼ tsp. salt
1/3 c. tomatoes

Brown beef in fat melted in frying pan. Add rest of ingredients, cover, and simmer for 30 minutes. Stir frequently.

Golden Corn Scallop

2 No. 2 cans corn (5 cups) cream style
2 c. milk
2 well beaten eggs
2 c. cracker crumbs
½ c. minced onion
6 Tbsp. chopped pimento
¼ c. butter or oleo
1 c. cracker crumbs

Heat corn & milk. Gradually stir in eggs. Add 2 c. crumbs, onion, & pimento. Pour in greased 2 qt. casserole. Pour 1 c. crumbs over with melted butter on top. Bake 1 hour at 350°. 12 Servings.

Dried Beef Hot Dish (Myrtle)

½ pkg. noodles
½ lb. dried beef
¼ c. butter or fat
1/3 c. flour
3 c. milk
1 green pepper, chopped
2 c. diced celery
1 jar sharp cheese
1 med. Onion, chopped

Boil noodles. Chip dried beef frizzle in hot water*. Drain & brown in butter. Parboil onions, pepper & celery. Save liquid, add noodles to beef, milk, cheese, onions, some of the liquid.

Bake 1 hour at 350° and cover with corn flakes and bake until flakes brown.

* This is actually what the original recipe says. You should simply break up the dried beef and soak in hot water for ten minutes or so.

149

MRS. PROBST'S BEANS

 1 lb Navy Beans
 1 tsp. salt
 2 Tbsp. molasses
 6 Tbsp. Light Brown Sugar
 1 scant tsp. Kitchen Bouquet (optional)
 ¼ lb Bacon, cut into 1" cubes or ham
 4 c. cold water

Wash but don't soak the beans. Place in thermizer (crock pot) utensil and add all other ingredients. Turn switch to simmer and cook for about 8 hours.

CHICKEN OR TUNA FISH SQUARES

 3 c. diced, cooked chicken (or tuna fish)
 1 c. cooked rice
 2 c. soft bread crumbs
 1/3 c. diced celery
 ¼ c. chopped pimento
 4 eggs, beaten
 2 tsp. salt
 ¼ tsp. poultry seasoning
 2 c. chicken broth

Combine rice, chicken, bread crumbs, celery, & pimento. To the beaten eggs add salt, poultry seasoning & broth (can use 2 chicken bouillon cubes dissolved in 2 c. hot water, cooled). Mix thoroughly. Stir in chicken mixture.

Bake in greased 9x9x2" baking dish in moderate oven (350°) for 55 min. Cut in squares and serve with mushroom sauce.

Mushroom Sauce:
Add 1/3 c. milk to 1 c. condensed mushroom soup. Head thoroughly.

Makes 6 to 8 servings.

CHICKEN HOT DISH (ANN'S)

One chicken stewed with onion. Take broth, cook 2 c. rice in it, also add chopped celery & green pepper. Add 1 can cream of mushroom soup thinned with cream. Pour over rice, also add boned chicken, pimento, blanched almonds. Bake 1 hour or so in 350° oven.

STEW

2 Tbsp. shortening
2 lbs beef chuck, cut in cubes
1 bay leaf
4 c. boiling water
4 drops hot pepper sauce
1 clove garlic
½ Tbsp. paprika
1 tsp. salt
3 potatoes (medium)
6 carrots, diced
10 small onions (halved)
½ c. flour

Melt shortening in deep frying pan. Brown meat in shortening. Pour off drippings. Add water, bay leaf, pepper sauce, garlic & other seasonings. Cover tightly and cook over low heat for 1 ½ hours.

Add potatoes, carrots in ½ inch pieces. Add onions. Stew ½ hour longer. Blend flour with ½ c. water, add to stew. If too thick, add additional water. Pour into heated casserole. Top with biscuits.

BISCUITS:

½ c. rich cornmeal
1 ½ c. sifted flour
3 tsp. baking powder
1 tsp. salt
¼ c. shortening
2/3 c. milk

Sift together dry ingredients. Mix in shortening. Add milk and stir until ingredients are dampened. Add a little more milk, if needed, to make a soft dough. Pat out dough, cut into biscuits. Place biscuits around edge of hot stew. Bake in 425° oven.

CHICKEN HOT DISH

1 c. uncooked spaghetti (cook & drain)
1 c. grated cheese
2 Tbsp. stuffed olives
1 or 2 c. cooked chicken
1 c. dry bread crumbs, cubed
¼ c. chopped green pepper or celery
1 ½ c. milk
3 eggs, beaten

Combine ingredients. Bake in greased pan for 1 hour in 350° oven.

Serve with condensed tomato soup on top (cut hot dish in squares, serve on plates).

CABBAGE HOT DISH
MIX TOGETHER:

  1 Tbsp. sugar
  2 Tbsp. flour
  1 c. sweet cream or milk
  1 medium cabbage

Pour cream over shredded cabbage. Cover top with slices of bacon. Bake 40 minutes in hot oven, 450°. Remove cover and brown.

TUNA TIMBALES (LOW CALORIE)

  2 eggs, beaten
  2 c. tuna fish
  ½ tsp. salt
  1/8 tsp. pepper
  ¼ tsp. celery salt
  1 tsp. paprika
  1 tsp. Worcestershire sauce
  1 Tbsp. lemon juice
  1 ½ c. milk
  1 c. Quaker oats (uncooked), quick or other

Combine all ingredients thoroughly and place in greased custard cups or loaf pan. Bake at 350° for 1 hour until set. Serve with mushroom sauce. Serves 6.

BAKED CHICKEN (VIRGINIA HERRICK)

    3 c. cooked chicken
    1 c. cooked rice
    1/3 c. diced celery
    ¼ c. pimentos
    4 eggs, beaten
    2 tsp. salt
    ¼ tsp. poultry seasoning
    2 c. chicken broth, or soup

Bake 55 minutes in 350° oven. Put on platter or else cut in squares, serve on plates with:

    1/3 c. milk
    1 can mushroom soup

SALMON AND CORN STEW

    2 Strips bacon (diced fine)
    1 peeled onion, sliced
    3 c. sliced, pared potatoes
    3 c. boiling water
    2 tsp. salt (scant)
    1 ½ c. whole kernel corn
    2 c. flaked salmon
    2 c. milk
    1 c. water

Sauté the bacon and onion until bacon is crisp. Add potatoes and boiling water. Cook 15 minutes or until potatoes are tender. Add salt, corn, salmon, milk and heat thoroughly.

CHICKEN HOT DISH

MIX LIKE GRAVY:

    4 Tbsp. butter
    1 Tbsp. onion
    4 Tbsp. flour
    1 c. chicken broth
    1 c. milk

STIR INTO GRAVY:

    1 c. grated cheese
    2 c. potato chips, crushed
    2 c. cooked chicken, cut up

Can add small can of mushrooms, if desired. Bake for ½ hour in 350° oven.

MEATS

HAM GELATIN

    1 no. 2.5 can Del Monte Fruit Cocktail
    2 Tbsp. unflavored gelatin
    2 Tbsp. vinegar
    ½ tsp. cinnamon
    1/8 tsp. cloves
    Syrup from fruit cocktail
    2 each 12 oz. cans ham luncheon meat chopped fine
    ½ c. chopped celery (fine)
    ¼ c. green pepper or olives, chopped fine
    ½ c. mayonnaise/salad dressing
    1 Tbsp. prepared mustard
    ½ tsp. salt

Arrange drained fruit cocktail in a loaf pan (9"x9"x3"). Add gelatin, vinegar, cinnamon, cloves to cold syrup. Dissolve in hot water. Carefully pour ¼ c. dissolved gelatin over fruit.

Mix ham, celery, green pepper (or olives). Mix salad dressing with mustard, salt & rest of dissolved gelatin.

Add to ham mixture. Mix well. Spread over fruit. Chill until firm, at least 4 hours.

Variety Meat Loaf

    1 ½ c. chopped, smoked ham
    2/3 c. chopped, uncooked veal
    1 c. chopped, uncooked beef
    1 Tbsp. chopped parsley
    2 Tbsp. chopped celery
    1 Tbsp. chopped onion
    ½ tsp. salt
    ¼ tsp. pepper
    1 egg or 2 yolks
    4 Tbsp. cream

Mix ingredients. Shape into a loaf 2" thick. Add ½ inch water. Cover and bake 1 hour in baking pan.

Bake in moderate oven 350° for 1 hour. Baste every 20 minutes.

American Chop Suey (Alice)

    Fry the following in butter:
    ¾ lb veal, cubed
    ¾ lb pork, cubed

Arrange ingredients in layers in buttered baking dish:

    Veal & Pork, fried
    1 package wide egg noodles, cooked in salt water
    1 can corn
    1 green pepper
    2 cans chicken soup, diluted

Bake slowly in 325° oven for 1 ½ hours. Add buttered crumbs and bake until crumbs brown.

HAM LOAF

1 lb smoked ham, ground
½ lb lean pork, ground
½ lb veal, ground
2 Tbsp. chopped green pepper
2 eggs, beaten slightly
1 c. milk
2 c. corn flakes, crumbled

Combine ingredients. Bake in greased loaf pan in moderate 350° oven for 1 hour.

SWISS STEAK EN CASSEROLE (ALICE)

¼ c. flour
2 tsp. salt
2 tsp. paprika
½ tsp. pepper
1 lb round steak, cut into serving pieces
1 clove garlic, cut in half
1/3 c. spry or Crisco
½ c. uncooked rice
2 c. canned or whole tomatoes
2 c. hot water

Mix flour with salt, paprika & pepper. Rub steak with garlic and then roll in flour. Brown onions in spry. Remove onions. Sear meat on both sides, but do not brown. Put in casserole greased with spry. Place onions, rice and tomatoes on meat. Add remainder of flour mixture to spry in skillet and blend until smooth. Add hot water gradually and cook until smooth. Strain over meat in casserole. Cook covered in moderate 350° oven for 1 ½ hour or until meat is tender.

BARBECUED FRANKFURTERS (ALICE)

Fry one medium onion cut fine in 2 Tbsp. butter
Add:
4 Tbsp. brown sugar
4 Tbsp. lemon juice
2 Tbsp. vinegar
1 c. catsup
½ c. water
1 tsp. dry mustard
Cook ½ hour.
Add 1 ½ lbs frankfurters, pricked.

Simmer ½ hour. Serve with buns or baked potatoes.

BARBECUED PORK CHOPS

6 or 8 lean pork chops
1 c. chili sauce
1 tsp. salt
1 tsp. celery salt
½ tsp. nutmeg
½ c. vinegar
½ c. water

Brown chops in hot fat in skillet. Place in casserole. Combine other
ingredients and pour sauce over pork chops. Cover and bake 1 hour at
350°.

MEAT BALLS (INEZ)

1 lb ground beef
6 Tbsp. raw rice
Salt & Pepper to taste

Mix all ingredients into balls. Place in casserole. Cover with 1 can tomato
soup & ¼ c. water. Bake in slow oven 325° for 1 ½ hour.

MEAT BALLS (ESTHER)

 2 lb. ground beef
 1 c. milk
 1 c. rolled corn flakes
 1 egg
 Salt & Pepper to taste

Mix well and roll into balls. Brown in butter. Put balls in casserole. Make a gravy in the frying pan with milk or water. Pour over balls. Bake 1 ½ hours in slow 325° oven.

SALMON STEAK GRILL

Cook sweet potatoes

Place slices of pineapple & sweet potatoes on a grill with salmon steak between them. Sprinkle each potato with a Tbsp. of brown sugar. Dot with butter. Season fish with salt, pepper and paprika. Add a dot of butter in the center of the fish.

No seasoning required on pineapple.

Place all in hot oven 375° oven. Cook 30 minutes or until steaks are done.

SALMON WITH CREOLE SAUCE

Melt 1 Tbsp. butter in saucepan. Brown 1 onion, 1 green pepper, both finely chopped. Add 1 can tomatoes, ½ tsp. chili powder & boil 10 minutes. Thicken with 1 Tbsp. flour, blended with tomato juice. Add 1 Tbsp. sugar.

Serve over cooked salmon steaks, or pour over steaks and bake.

CHICKEN SAUCE

½ lb butter or oleo, melted
Juice of 2 lemons or 5 Tbsp. real lemon
2 tsp. Worchester sauce
1 tsp. Kitchen Bouquet (optional)

Mix well and pour over cut up chicken in pan. Sprinkle with paprika.
Baste chicken several times. Add a little pepper & salt.

Bake in 350° oven.

GOLDEN FISH FILLETS

2 lbs fresh or frozen fish fillets
¼ c. salad oil
2 tsp. vinegar
2 tsp. chopped onion
2 tsp. paprika
Dash of pepper
2 tsp. salt
1 c. flour
2 well-beaten eggs
1 c. bread crumbs

Wipe fillets with a damp cloth. Cut into pieces. Mix salad oil, onion,
paprika & pepper. Dip fish into mixture. Let stand 1 hour in deep pan,
turning frequently. Drain. Add salt to flour. Roll fish in it. Drop fish in egg
then into bread crumbs. Fry in deep fat, turn only once.

TARTAR SAUCE

¾ c. mayonnaise
1 tsp. chopped onion
1/8 c. drained pickle relish

Mix.

SANDWICH SPREAD

1 c. spam
6 hard boiled eggs
3 carrots, grated
1 onion, chopped fine
1 green pepper, chopped fine
1 pint Miracle Whip
2 Tbsp. sugar
2 Tbsp. vinegar
1 tsp. salt

Mix all ingredients. Keep chilled until used.

JUICY MEAT LOAF

1 ½ lb ground beef
¾ c. Quaker Oats, quick or old fashioned
2 eggs, beaten
¼ c. chopped onions
2 tsp. salt
¼ tsp. pepper
1 c. tomato juice

Bake in 350° oven for 1 hour. Let stand 5 minutes before slicing.

For meat balls, omit eggs in meat loaf recipe. Make 16 meatballs. Roll in flour, brown in hot shortening. Add 1 c. tomato sauce puree. Simmer 20-25 min.

BARBECUE SAUCE (FOR VEAL CHOPS)

4 shoulder veal chops, ¾" thick
4 Tbsp. lard or shortening
3 Tbsp. soy sauce
3 Tbsp. catsup
1 Tbsp. vinegar
¼ tsp. sugar (optional)
¼ tsp. pepper
1 clove garlic, chopped fine
1 Tbsp. Worchester sauce

Brown chops in shortening, slowly. Combine the other ingredients. Beat. Pour over chops and cook for 1 hour, turn chops over once in a while. Simmer slowly.

PICKLES

SWEET DILL (MRS. RULE)

3 quarts water to 1 c. salt for brine

Put a layer of cucumbers, 1 layer of dill and 1 layer of grape leaves in jar.

Use all cucumbers, cover with the brine. Let stand 14 days. Take out and wipe dry. Slice lengthwise and put in jars. Pour over hot syrup:

1 c. vinegar
1 c. sugar
whole spices (careful of red peppers)
Small chunk alum

Let stand overnight in jars. Next morning, drain off juice. Add 1 c. sugar to every cup of juice. Let boil. Pour over cucumbers hot and seal.

PICKLED BEETS

2 c. sugar
2 c. water
2 c. strong vinegar
1 tsp. cloves
1 tsp. allspice
1 Tbsp. cinnamon
1 thinly sliced lemon, if desired

Boil beets in mixture. Put into jars (per canning directions).

SPICED BEETS (LAURA)

BOIL TOGETHER:

½ c. water
½ c. vinegar
1 Tbsp. brown sugar
¼ tsp. salt
½ tsp. cinnamon
¼ tsp. cloves

Pour over two cups diced beets. Put into jars (per canning directions).

PICKLED BEANS
BOIL:

6 c. vinegar
1 c. brown sugar
1 tsp. salt
½ tsp. pepper
1 tsp. allspice
1 stick cinnamon
1 Tbsp. whole cloves
4 Qts. green or yellow beans

Cook beans in boiling water (salted) until tender (1 tsp. salt to each qt. of water). Drain, pack in jars, pour boiling syrup over, seal hot. Makes 8 quarts.

CHILLI SAUCE

2 doz. ripe tomatoes

3 green peppers (small)

3 onions

½ c. vinegar

2 tsp. salt

1 tsp. cloves

1 tsp. nutmeg

1 tsp. ginger

1 tsp. allspice

Boil all slowly for 3 hours. If tomatoes are too juicy, drain off some of the liquid before adding other ingredients.

TOMATO CATSUP (MRS. RULE)

2 qts ripe tomatoes, boil and strain

2 tsp. salt

2 c. vinegar

2/3 c. sugar

Mix with tomatoes, boil until thick. Pour into hot bottles and seal.

STRING BEAN PICKLES

1/3 c. vinegar

3/4 c. sugar

Bag of mixed spices (pickling spices)

Boil all together. Cook beans in salt water until tender. Fill jars with hot beans, pour hot syrup over them and seal.

INDIAN RELISH

50 small or 25 large green tomatoes, chopped and drained

8 onions

4 green peppers

4 red peppers

4 c. vinegar

4 c. sugar

4 Tbsp. salt

2 Tbsp. white mustard seed

2 Tbsp. celery seed.

Boil all together until clear. Fill jars and seal.

CHOW CHOW (MRS. KING)

2 heads cabbage

1 peck green tomatoes

6 onions

2 peppers

Chop all fine and boil for 20 minutes with 1 pint vinegar and ½ c. salt. Drain thoroughly, then place in kettle with 3 pints of vinegar and 3 lbs of sugar:

1 tsp. cloves

1 tsp. allspice

1 tsp. cinnamon

Boil until tender. Fill jars and seal.

5 DAY CHUNK PICKLE (DOROTHY)

    2 gals cucumbers (not over 2 inches in diameter)
    2 qts cold water
    1 c. salt
    Cover cucumbers, let stand for 24 hours.

SECOND DAY: drain, but do not rinse. Add 1 gal of boiling water. Let stand overnight.

THIRD DAY: Drain pickles, cover with solution:

    1 part white vinegar
    1 part water

FOURTH DAY: Drain pickles, make syrup:

    2 qts white vinegar
    3 c. sugar
    2 Tbsp. mixed pickling spices

Pour over pickles, cover pickles with syrup. Cover with weighted lid after they cool.

FIFTH DAY: Drain syrup from pickles, add 3 c. sugar. Bring to boiling point. Pack pickles in jars lined with grape leaves. Pour boiling syrup over pickles and seal at once.

Makes 5 pints.

PIES

PUMPKIN PIE

    2/3 c. sugar

    1 tsp. salt

    3 eggs (can use 2 large ones)

    1 ½ Tbsp. flour

    1 ½ c. stewed pumpkin

    ½ tsp. cinnamon

    ½ tsp. ginger

    2 Tbsp. molasses

    1 c. milk

Fill single crust pie shell. Bake slow at 350°.

PEACH PIE

    4 c. sliced peaches

    1 ½ c. sugar

    1 tsp. cinnamon

    ½ tsp. cloves

    1/8 tsp. salt

    2 Tbsp. flour

    3 Tbsp. water

    2 Tbsp. lemon juice

    3 Tbsp. butter

Blend peaches, sugar, spices & flour. Put into pice shell, add water, and juice, cover with crust. Make 4 slits in top crust. Bake 40 minutes in a moderate oven, 350°.

Banana Kremel Pie

Slice bananas in shell, put vanilla kremel over it and merignue on top. Brown in oven at 350 degrees.

[Amy's note: Kremel was a dessert product like Jell-O pudding, so you should be able to substitute any vanilla pudding for the Kremel in this recipe.]

Mince Meat Filling

Makes 2 Quarts Mince Meat (2 pies)

> 2 lbs lean beef
> 4 c. water
> 1 lb chopped suet
> 3 c. chopped apples
> 3 c. cider
> 2 c. shopped raisins
> 1 c. chopped currants
> ½ c. chopped candied orange peel
> 1 c. candied pineapple
> 4 c. sugar
> ½ c. molasses
> ½ c. lemon juice
> 1 c. grape juice
> 2 Tbsp. salt
> ½ tsp. pepper
> 2 Tbsp. cinnamon
> 1 Tbsp. cloves
> 2 tsp. nutmeg

Add water to meat. Cover and cook very slowly 2 hours. Chop and add with stock to rest of ingredients. Cook slowly for 1 ½ hours. Stir frequently. Pour into jars and seal.

LEMON PIE

Mix together four Tbsp. of cornstarch, and 1 c. sugar. Pour over this mixture 1 1/8 c. of boiling water and boil for 5 minutes. Stir constantly.

Add 1 ½ Tbsp. butter, juice of 1 lemon, grated rind. Pour this mixture over 2 well beaten egg yolks. Use whites of eggs for meringue. Bake at 350° until done.

CHERRY PIE

    One can unsweetened cherries
    1 c. sugar
    6 tsp. cornstarch
    ½ tsp. lemon extract
    1 tsp. butter
    Pinch of salt

PASTRY:

    1 c. flour
    ½ c. shortening
    ½ tsp. salt
    1/3 c. water

Drain juice from cherries, place over fire. When juice boils, add sugar mixed with cornstarch. Take from fire, add butter, pour over cherries and let cool white making crust.

Bake in 350° oven until nicely browned.

MRS. BRONSON'S PUMPKIN PIE

2 eggs
2 c. milk
2/3 c. brown sugar
1 tsp. cinnamon
½ tsp. salt
1 ½ c. pumpkin
½ tsp. ginger

Make filling, place in single crust pie shell and bake at 350° until done.

BUTTER SCOTCH PIE

1 ½ c. boiling water
1 egg yolk
1 c. dark brown sugar
3 tsp. flour
Pinch of salt
1 tsp. vanilla
1 Tbsp. butter

Frost with egg whites . Pour in single crust pie shell and bake at 350° until done.

PECAN PIE

1 unbaked pie shell
¼ c. butter or oleo
½ c. sugar
3 whole eggs
1 c. dark brown syrup
1 Tbsp. lemon juice
1 c. coarsely chopped pecans
1 tsp. vanilla
½ c. whipped cream (optional)

Line pie plate with crust, 1 c. flour, 6 tsp. butter or oleo, ¼ tsp. salt, 2 tsp. cold water. Brush with slightly beaten egg. Cream butter or oleo, with sugar. Stir in eggs, syrup, lemon juice, add vanilla, and mix until well blended. Fold in nuts, turn out on to crust. Bake in very hot oven at 450 degrees for 10 minutes. Reduce heat to 350 degrees and bake for 30 minutes or until filling is set. Serve with whipped cream.

DATE PIE

Mix in double boiler.

1 ¾ c. milk
¼ c. sugar

Stir in paste of 2 Tbsp. cornstarch, 1 Tbsp. flour and ¼ c. milk.

Return to heat, stirring constantly. Cook 10 minutes until thick. Stir a little of the hot mixture into 2 egg yolks beaten well. Add to hot mixture and cook 2 minutes. Blend in ½ Tbsp. butter. Remove from heat. Cool. Stir in 1 tsp. vanilla and ¾ c. chopped dates.

Pour into cool pie shell, cool and serve with whipped cream.

SOUR CREAM PIE

1 c. sugar
1 c. raisins, pour boiling water over them. Let stand little while,
then drain and add:
2 eggs
1 c. sour cream
2 Tbsp. vinegar
Dashes of nutmeg, cloves, allspice, cinnamon, and salt

Mix, pour into pie shell and bake in moderate 350° oven until set.

DUTCH APPLE PIE

6-8 apples
1 c. sweet or sour cream
½ c. sugar
1 c. brown sugar
½ tsp. cinnamon
3 Tbsp. flour

Quarter apples. Mix brown sugar, white sugar, cinnamon and flour. Put half of mixture in bottom of unbaked pie shell. Add apples. Arrange in layers. Mix cream with remaining flour and sugar and pour over top. Put in hot oven at 450°. After 10 minutes, reduce heat to 325°. Bake pie about 45 minutes or until apples are transparent. Serve hot or cold.

LEMON CHIFFON PIE

Soften 1 Tbsp. gelatin in ½ c. cold water. Put 4 egg yolks, 1 c. sugar, dash of salt, 1/3 c. lemon juice, grated lemon rind of ½ lemon in double boiler. Mix well. Cook over boiling water until thick and foamy, beating with rotary beater 3 min. Remove from heat. Add gelatin. Cool. Beat 4 egg whites stiff, beat in ½ c. sugar gradually. Fold into gelatin mixture. Put in pie shells. Chill until filling is set.

GRAHAM CRACKER PIE

 18 Graham crackers rolled fine
 ¼ c. melted butter
 ¼ c. melted Oleo (or can use all butter)
 ¼ c. sugar

Roll crackers, add melted shortening, then sugar. Mix with spoon then press in pie tin (reserve 2 Tbsp. for topping).

FILLING

 3 egg yolks beaten
 ½ c. sugar
 2 c. milk
 2 Tbsp. cornstarch

Boil until thick. Pour over pie crust. Use beaten egg whites for top. Sprinkle with graham cracker crumbs and brown

PINEAPPLE PIE (ADAH SHIMER)

Heat 1 ½ c. milk. Mix ½ c. sugar, 1/8 tsp. salt, 2 Tbsp. cornstarch and slowly add to hot milk and cook in double boiler until thick (about 40 minutes). Pour into 2 egg yolks (beaten) and return to double boiler. Cook until eggs thicken (about 3 minutes).

Cool.

Add 1 c. well-drained crushed pineapple & ½ tsp. vanilla. Pour mixture into crust. Cover with meringue made of 2 stiffly beaten egg whites and 2 Tbsp. powdered sugar.

Brown quickly in hot oven (425°).

MINCE MEAT PIE FILLING

    4 lb lean meat, chopped fine
    2 lb suet
    8 lb juicy apples, chopped fine
    4 lb seedless raisins
    2 lbs currants
    1 lb citron, chopped
    1 lb brown sugar
    1 pint sorgum or syrup
    2 pints sweet cider
    1 pint boiled cider

Mix well & heat well.

    1 tsp. salt
    1 tsp. pepper
    1 tsp. mace
    1 tsp. allspice
    4 tsp. cinnamon
    2 grated nutmegs
    1 tsp. cloves

Put all together and boil 5 minutes and put in prepared canning jars. Boil 30 minutes or cold pack.

PINEAPPLE CHIFFON PIE

    1 c. sugar
    4 egg yolks
    1 c. water
    1 small can of pineapple

Warm and add ½ amount of sugar. Add 2 heaping tsp. flour or cornstarch, dash of salt. Fold in egg whites and ½ of sugar. Put in backed pie shell. Refrigerate.

CRANBERRY PIE

½ c. sugar
1 c. flour
1 tsp. baking powder
1 c. cranberries
1 Tbsp. melted butter
½ c. milk

Cream sugar and butter. Add milk and dry ingredients. Add cranberries and bake in prepared, single crust pie tin at 400°.

Serve hot with butter sauce.

BUTTER SAUCE

1/3 c. sugar
¼ c. butter
1 c. cream

Cook in double boiler. Remove from fire and add a few drops of coloring or cranberries into sauce.

Cut pie into pieces and pour over while sauce is hot.

PUMPKIN PIE

Pastry for one-crust pie
1 ¾ c. mashed, cooked pumpkin
1 ½ c. milk
2 eggs
2/3 c. brown sugar, firmly packed
½ tsp. salt
½ tsp. ginger
½ tsp. nutmeg
¼ tsp. cloves
1 tsp. cinnamon

Beat ingredients together with a rotary beater. Pour into pastry-lined 9" pie pan. Bake 40-45 min or until a silver knife inserted into filling comes out clean. Center will be soft but will set later. Bake in a moderately hot oven, 400°.

Note: to save on sugar, use 1/3 c. honey and 1/3 c. brown sugar in place of 2/3 c. brown sugar.

LIBBY'S PUMPKIN PIE

2 eggs, slightly beaten
1 can Libby's Pumpkin
¾ c. sugar
½ tsp. salt
1 tsp. cinnamon
½ tsp. ginger
¼ tsp. cloves
1 2/3 c. evaporated milk
1 ea 9" unbaked pie shell

Mix all ingredients. Pour into pie shell. Bake in hot oven at 425° for 15 minutes. Reduce heat to 350° and bake 45 minutes or until a knife inserted in center comes out clean.

ORANGE PIE

Bake pastry shell and cool. May also use graham cracker crust.

30 marshmallows, melted in double boiler with ¾ c. orange juice. When cool, whip 1 c. heavy cream. Add to first mixture with a little grated orange rind. Put in shell. Let set.

You can sprinkle nuts and grated chocolate on top (or both).

PINEAPPLE PIE (TWO CRUSTS)

1 No. 2 can grated pineapple, juice and all

Put into prepared pie pan/bottom crust. Sprinkle top with 1 Tbsp. flour, generous amount of butter, 1/3 c. sugar. Put on top crust. Bake at 350° until crust is brown.

PINEAPPLE FLUFF PIE

Beat until fluffy:

> 4 egg yolks
> ¼ c. sugar

Dissolve 1 package lemon Jell-O in 1 c. boiling water. Add to first mixture. Beat well and cool. Add 1 c. crushed pineapple and again beat until syrupy. Beat 4 egg whites until stiff. Add ¼ c. sugar. Fold into first mixture.

Pour into pie shell.

Chill and serve with whipped cream.

ICE CREAM AND CHOCOLATE PASTRY

1 c. sifted flour
½ tsp. salt
4 tsp. cocoa
½ c. shortening
¾ tsp. vanilla
1 or 2 Tbsp. cold water

Mix like any pie crust. Turn onto wax paper. Let stand 15 minutes. Then line pie pan and back at 450° for 12 or 15 minutes.

When cold, fill with 1 quart strawberry ice cream. Top with meringue listed below.

MERINGUE

3 egg whites
1 tsp. salt

Beat. Then add:

¾ tsp. cream of tartar
1 tsp. vanilla

Brown in oven at 450°.

PLAIN PASTRY

3 c. flour
1 tsp. salt
1 c. shortening
½ to 2/3 c. cold water

Mix. Turn mixture onto wax paper. Chill for easier handling. Roll out.

Sour Cream Pie

1 egg, beaten well
1 c. raisins, chopped fine
¾ c. sugar
½ tsp. cinnamon
1 c. thick sour milk or buttermilk

Mix well. Heat mixture on stove in a double boiler. Put in a 2-crust pie shell. Bake in moderate over (350°).

Cocoanut Pie Crust

Spread butter evenly on bottom of pie pan.

Sprinkle cocoanut evenly into pan and pat into butter.

Bake at 350° oven for 10 or 12 minutes until golden brown. Cool.

Fill shell with favorite Jell-O pudding or pie filling.

Peach Pie (Fresh Peaches)

¾ c. sugar (1/4 brown)
2 or 3 Tbsp. flour
¼ tsp. cinnamon
5 c. sliced fresh peaches
2 Tbsp. butter or Oleo

Combine sugar, flour & cinnamon. Add peaches, mix lightly. Dot with butter. Put into pie shells with lattice top. Bake at 400° for 40-50 minutes.

CANNED PEACH PIE

    1 Tbsp. corn starch
    1 c. syrup
    1 Tbsp. lemon juice
    1 Tbsp. butter or Oleo
    ¼ tsp. cinnamon

Take cornstarch and add to a small amount of peach syrup to make a paste. Mix with remaining syrup. Cook over low heat until thick, stirring constantly. Add peaches and place in prepared pie pan. Make a lattice top pie crust. Bake at 400° for 40-50 minutes.

FUDGE PIE (DELORES NAGEL)

    Beat 1 c. sugar & ½ c. butter
    Beat 2 egg yolks
    Melt 2 squares chocolate
    ½ c. flour
    1 tsp. vanilla
    Beat 2 egg whites with ½ tsp. salt

Fold egg whites into first mixture. Put in greased pie plate.

Bake at 325° for 30 minutes.

Top with ice cream.

Karo Pecan Pie

2 eggs beaten
1 c. Karo syrup
1/8 tsp. salt
1 tsp. vanilla
1 c. sugar
2 Tbsp. melted butter or Oleo margarine
1 c. Pecan meats

FROSTING

2 egg whites
½ c. Karo syrup
½ c. sugar
1 tsp. vanilla

Mix pie ingredients, pour into prepared pie shell and bake at 350° until done.

Beat frosting until fluffy. Frost when cooled.

Angel Cream Pie

4 egg whites, beaten stiff
Add ¼ tsp. cream of tartar
Beat thoroughly
Add 1 c. sugar.
Beat some more.

Grease (well) one 9" pie tin and put above mixture in. Bake in a very slow oven 1 hour (275°). After 15 min, increase heat to 300°.

4 egg yolks, beat thoroughly until lemon color
Add 1 c. sugar.
Beat well.
Add juice & rink of 1 lemon

Cook in double boiler until thick. Cool both crust & this custard.

Whip ½ pint of whipping cream & spread part of cream over crust. Then add custard & remaining whipped cream.

Chill 24 hours before serving.

Note, you can bake the first mixture in a long pan, but make double the amount of custard if you do.

CREAMY CHEESE PIE

1 package (8 oz) cream cheese, softened
1/3 c. sugar (or sugar substitute)
½ c. sour cream
1 tsp. vanilla
1 container (4 oz) Cool Whip, thawed
1 prepared 8" graham cracker crust

Beat cheese until smooth. Gradually beat in sugar. Blend in sour cream and vanilla. Fold in Cool Whip whipped topping. Blend thoroughly. Spoon into crust and chill until set, about 4 hours. Serve topped with Cherry Pie filling, if desired.

BERLINE'S PECAN PIE (BERLINE BALDWIN)
Makes 2 pies

    4 eggs, beaten
    1 box light brown sugar
    2 Tbsp. corn meal
    1 Tbsp. flour
    ½ stick melted butter
    1 tsp. vanilla
    2 to 2 ½ c. pecans

Mix the first 6 ingredients, then add the nuts. Pour into prepared pie tins (you can use store bought pie crust) for 1-crust pies. Bake at 350° for one hour.

PRESERVES

RHUBARB JELLY PRESERVES

      6 c. rhubarb, cut fine (let stand overnight)

      6 c. sugar

Boil 5 minutes. Add 2 packages strawberry Jell-O and a small can of crushed pineapple.

Boil 15 minutes.

Place in sterilized, prepared jars.

RHUBARB JELLY

      4 c. rhubarb cut fine

      4 c. sugar

      1 package strawberry Jell-O

Mix. Boil hard for 15 minutes.

Place in sterilized, prepared jars.

SALADS

GOLDEN APPLE MOLD

    1 envelope Knox Sparkling Gelatin
    ¼ c. cold water
    1 Tbsp. sugar
    1 Tbsp. lemon juice
    1 tsp. grated orange rind
    ½ c. orange juice
    1 c. hot, sweetened applesauce
    ¼ tsp. salt
    2 egg whites
    1 c. orange sections

Soften gelatin in cold water and dissolve over hot water. Mix lemon juice, orange juice, salt, sugar, orange rind and applesauce. Add dissolved gelatin, stirring thoroughly. Cool, and when mixture begins to thicken, fold in stiffly beaten egg whites. Pour into square pan that has been rinsed in cold water. Chill until firm. Serve in squares and garnish with orange sections and custard sauce.

DEVILED EGGS (4)

    1 tsp. vinegar
    ¼ tsp. dry mustard
    salt and cayenne to taste

Boil 4 eggs until hard-boiled. Cool and peel. Cut in half length-wise and scoop out yolk. Mix ingredients with the yolks. Add enough melted butter to handle mixture. Replace yolk mixture in hollows.

SALAD (BLACK CHERRY)

    1 pkg Cherry Jell-O
    Bing Cherries, pitted
    Small marshmallows
    Bananas

Mix, chill and serve on a bed of lettuce.

CRANBERRY SALAD

    1 pkg lemon Jell-O
    1 ½ c. hot water
    ½ c. celery, cut fine
    ½ c. crushed pineapple, drained
    1 c. cranberry sauce, cooked thick

Mix. Let set. Serve with dressing.

FRUIT SALAD

    1 medium-sized can pineapple, cut in pieces
    10 or 12 marshmallows, cut in pieces
    2 bananas, diced

Mix. Serve with dressing.

EGG SALAD

    6 eggs, hard boiled
    ½ c. cucumbers, diced
    ½ c. sweet peppers, diced
    Pinch of celery salt
    Pinch of paprika

Mix with mayonnaise dressing.

SALAD DRESSING FOR FRUIT

¼ c. pineapple juice
¼ c. lemon juice
1/3 c. sugar
2 eggs
Pinch of salt

Mix juice, sugar and salt together. Add eggs. Boil 2 minutes.

VEAL SALAD

2 c. diced, cooked veal
4 hard boiled eggs, diced
1/3 c. chopped celery
3 Tbsp. chopped pimentos
2 Tbsp. chopped sweet pickles
½ tsp. salt
¼ tsp. paprika
½ c. salad dressing

Mix and chill. Serve on a crisp lettuce leaf.

MOCK CHICKEN SALAD

2 c. cold roast pork, cut in cubes
1 c. celery cut in small pieces
4 olives, stoned and chopped
½ red pepper

Mix pork cubes, celery and olives. Add ½ of pepper which has been washed, parboiled and seeds removed, then cut in thin strips.

Moisten with mayonnaise. Mound in salad bowl. Garnish with celery strips and remaining pepper.

HEALTHY SALAD

> 2 carrots
> 1 apple
> 1 c. shredded cabbage
> ½ c. French or boiled dressing

Mix and eat.

VEGETABLE SALAD

> 1 c. cooked peas
> ½ c. cooked carrots
> 3 Tbsp. chopped celery
> 1 Tbsp. chopped onion
> ½ c. diced beets
> 2 Tbsp. chopped pickles
> 1/3 tsp. salt
> ¼ tsp. paprika
> 1/3 c. French Dressing

Mix and serve.

FRUIT SALAD

> 1 c. sliced bananas
> 2 Tbsp. lemon juice
> ½ c. diced celery
> ¼ tsp. salt
> 1 c. diced pineapple
> ½ c. diced peaches

Mix and chill ingredients. Serve on a bed of lettuce.

BOILED DRESSING

¼ tsp. salt
1 tsp. mustard
1 ½ Tbsp. sugar
2 Tbsp. flour
1 egg or 2 egg yolks
1 ½ Tbsp. melted butter
3/4 c. milk
¼ c. vinegar
Few grains cayenne pepper

Mix and boil until thick.

MAYONNAISE

1 egg
Dash of pepper
1 pint Wesson Oil
1 tsp. sugar
1 tsp. salt
1 tsp. mustard
2 Tbsp. lemon juice or vinegar

Put all ingredients except oil into a blender or food processor. Whip while pouring oil in. When all the oil is in, whip another second or so.

BEAN SALAD

    1 can French cut green beans
    1 can Wax beans
    1 can Kidney beans
    ½ c. chopped green pepper (fine)
    ½ c. chopped onion (fine)
    ½ c. vinegar
    ½ c. sugar
    ½ c. salad oil (mix oil, vinegar & sugar together)
    1 tsp. salt
    ½ tsp. pepper

Drain beans. Drain kidney beans and rinse. Add onion and pepper. Pour vinegar mixture over vegetables and let stand in refrigerator several hours.

TUNA FISH SALAD

    1 ½ c. tuna fish, flaked
    1 ½ c. diced celery
    2 hard cooked eggs, diced
    ½ tsp. salt
    ¼ tsp. paprika
    ½ c. salad dressing

Mix. Chill and serve on a bed of lettuce.

BANANA SALAD

Peel bananas, cut lengthwise, and brush with slightly beaten egg whites. Then sprinkle with peanuts. Place on lettuce leaf. Garnish with cherries or walnut halves, or marshmallows.

Serve with mayonnaise with ½ c. shipped cream added. Must be served within a very short time.

MAYONNAISE SALAD DRESSING

½ tsp. mustard
½ tsp. sugar
½ tsp. salt
1 egg yolk
1 Tbsp. vinegar
¾ c. salad oil
1 Tbsp. lemon juice
Few grains of cayenne pepper

Mix well.

PARIESIENNE DRESSING

1 tsp. salt
1 tsp. dry mustard
1 tsp. sugar
1 tsp. paprika
¼ tsp. cayenne
1 c. Wesson oil
2 Tbsp. tomato catsup
¼ c. vinegar

Put all ingredients except oil into a blender. Whip while pouring oil into it. When all the oil is gone, whip another few seconds.

Hot Potato Salad

6 potatoes, med size, cooked
1 onion, minced
½ c. celery, diced
½ green pepper, diced
½ c. bacon, cut into small squares
2 Tbsp. sugar
3 Tbsp. flour
¼ c. vinegar
1 ¼ c. water
1 Tbsp. salt
Pepper

Cut cooked potatoes in slices. Place bacon in a large pan, brown. Mix flour with a small amount of cold water to make a smooth paste. When bacon is brown, add the remaining cold water, vinegar, sugar, salt, dash of pepper, and the flour paste. Stir until the sauce boils well, then add the potatoes, onion, celery, and green pepper.

Allow salad to stand in a warm place for 15 min to season. Serve warm. Hard-cooked eggs are often added to this salad.

Golden Glow Salad

1 c. boiling water
1 c. pineapple juice
1 tsp. vinegar
½ tsp. salt
Crushed pineapple
1 c. grated carrots

Pour boiling water over 1 pkg lemon Jell-O. Add pineapple juice. Let cool.

Add carrots, pineapple, salt.

Use ½ c. miracle whip or homemade salad dressing and ½ c. whipped cream to top.

APPLE SALAD

    1 c. carrots, cut fine
    1 c. apple, cut fine (leave peeling on)
    1 c. chopped almonds

Mix and serve.

BOILED SALAD DRESSING

    Boil the following together until thick:
    4 eggs, beaten
    3 tsp. flour
    1 c. vinegar
    2 c. water
    ½ tsp. salt
    1 tsp. mustard
    1 tsp. butter
    ½ c. sugar (or more, if desired)

Let cool.

CRANBERRY RING

    1 pkg Jell-O
    ¾ c. hot water
    2 c. cranberries, raw, ground
    1 c. diced celery
    1 apple, diced
    ½ c. nut meats
    ¼ c. sugar

Mix ground berries with sugar. Add to the rest of the mixture. Let cool until set.

Salad for 8

Put through food chopper:

8 hard boiled eggs

6 raw carrots

1 small onion

Also, cooked beets & celery, if desired

Juice of 1 lemon

1 ½ pt. of lemon or lime Jell-O (Use ½ water on package of Jell-O.)

1 c. mayonnaise and a pinch of salt. Add Jell-O last.

Serve on a lettuce leaf.

Spring Salad

12 spears of cooked asparagus

1/3 c. cooked peas

1/3 c. cooked carrots

3 Tbsp. chopped celery

1 tsp. chopped green peppers

½ tsp. chopped onion

1/8 tsp. salt

1/8 tsp. paprika

4 Tbsp. French dressing

2 Tbsp. mayonnaise

Mix vegetables, salt, paprika, French dressing. Chill. Serve on a lettuce leaf with a dollop of mayonnaise.

Chilled Diced Fruit

1 c. grapefruit, diced
1 c. pineapple, diced
1 c. pears, diced
1 c. seeded grapes
¼ c. sugar
½ c. water
1 Tbsp. lemon juice

Mix all ingredients. Chill for 1 hour or longer. Serve in glass cups.

Salad Dressing

1 part vinegar
2 part oil
Salt, pepper, onion or garlic

Shake/mix well.

Salad Dressing (Girls' Club)

2 bottles of catsup
4 tsp. paprika
4 tsp. salt
Juice of 4 lemons
5 ½ c. Mazola corn oil
1 ¾ c. syrup
1 large onion, grated fine
2 c. vinegar

Mix and bottle in sterilized jars.

CRANBERRY SALAD (DELORES NAGEL)

15 Marshmallows
½ lb cranberries, ground
1 small can crushed pineapple
1 c. sugar, added to the berries
1 c. whipped cream

Grind raw cranberries and add sugar. Then add pineapple. Cut marshmallows into small pieces and add them and the whipped cream.

FROZEN GRAPE SALAD

2 each 3 oz. packages cream cheese
2 Tbsp. mayonnaise
2 Tbsp. pineapple syrup
24 marshmallows, quartered
1 can pineapple bits, drained
1 c. heavy cream, whipped
2 c. grapes, halved & seeded

Soften cream cheese and blend with mayonnaise. Add marshmallows & pineapple bits. Fold in whipped cream and halved grapes. Pour into refrigerator tray. Freeze until firm. Cut in squares.

Serves eight.

BEST CRANBERRY SALAD

4 c. fresh cranberries
2 c. sugar
2 c. red grapes
1 can crushed pineapple tidbits, drained
½ c. chopped nuts
1 c. cream, whipped

Put cranberries through grinder. Sprinkle with sugar. Let stand overnight and then drain. Use this juice for fruit punch.

Cut grapes in halves. Remove the seeds. Add grapes, pineapple & nuts to drained cranberry mixture. Fold in whipped cream. Garnish with pineapple rings cut in half & whole grapes to make a flower.

Serves 6.

WALDORF DATE SALAD

½ c. chopped celery
½ c. pitted, chopped dates
4 marshmallows, quartered
½ c. cooked dressing
2 c. diced apples
½ c. broken nut meats

Combine celery, dates, marshmallows & cooked dressing. Chill thoroughly. Just before serving, add apples and nuts.

6 servings.

COOKED DRESSING

2 Tbsp. flour
2 Tbsp. sugar
1 tsp. salt
1 tsp. dry mustard
Few grains of cayenne
1 ½ tsp. butter
2 slightly beaten eggs
¾ c. milk
¼ c. vinegar

Mix dry ingredients. Add egg yolk and milk. Cook in double boiler until thick, stirring constantly. Add vinegar & butter. Mix well.

Makes 1 c.

CRANBERRY STARS (GIRLS' CLUB)

1 c. ground fresh cranberries
1 c. sugar
1 package lemon Jell-O
1 c. hot water
1 c. pineapple syrup
1 c. crushed pineapple, well drained
½ c. nut meats
1 c. chopped celery
1 c. red grapes, cut up (optional)

Combine cranberries and sugar.

Dissolve gelatin in hot water. Add pineapple syrup and chill until partially set. Add cranberry mixture, pineapple, nuts, celery and grapes. Chill.

Serve with a dollop of mayonnaise.

Serves 6.

PINEAPPLE SALAD

1 can crushed pineapple
1 c. sugar
1 tsp. salt
2 Tbsp. flour
1 egg
2 Tbsp. lemon juice
1 tsp. grated lemon peel
¾ c. whipping cream
¼ lb marshmallows

Drain pineapple, keep syrup. Combine sugar, salt & flour with syrup in saucepan. Add egg. Mix thoroughly. Stir in pineapple juice. Cook, stirring constantly until thick and smooth.

Remove from heat. Add lemon juice & peel. Cover and chill.

Whip cream stiff. Add to mixture. Fold in marshmallows (cut into quarters). Also add pineapple. May also add ¼ c. Maraschino cherries. Chill.

DOROTHY PFIELSTICKER'S SALAD DRESSING

1 c. Mazola corn oil
½ c. sugar
1/3 c. catsup (or more)
¼ c. vinegar
1 tsp. salt
1 tsp. paprika

Mix well and serve.

HAM SALAD

> 1 package lemon Jell-O
> 1 c. boiling water
> Mix, cool and add:
> 1 c. cream, whipped
> 1 c. mayonnaise or Miracle Whip
> ¼ c. ground sweet pickle
> 1 Tbsp. pimentos, cut fine
> 1 c. or ½ lb. ham, cut fine
> (can also add some grated carrot)

Mix and serve.

LIME JELL-O SALAD (EFFIE)

> 1 Package Lime Jell-O
> 1 C. hot water, add Jell-O and dissolve
> 1 c. Ginger ale
> 2 Apples cut up fine, leaving the skin on
> ½ c. Chopped celery

Mix and add anything else you like such as grated carrots, nut meats or olives.

FRUIT SALAD

> 1 can Mandarin oranges, diced
> 1 c. pineapple syrup & pineapple bits
> 1 c. small marshmallows
> 1 c. cocoanut (shredded)
> 1 c. sour cream

Mix all the night before. Serve on a bed of lettuce.

CAPE COD CRANBERRY SALAD

    1 c. leftover chicken
    1 c. cubed cranberry jelly
    1 c. celery, chopped
    1 Tbsp. lemon juice
    Salt & pepper to taste

Mix all ingredients with ½ c. mayonnaise.

Chill. Serve on a bed of lettuce. Garnish with pickles, olives, parsley or whatever you like.

VEGETABLES

RED CABBAGE (MRS. IRENE PADGETT)

    1/3 stick butter, melted in a saucepan
    1 med. Onion, diced finely

Sauté the onion in the butter.

Wash a head of red cabbage and cut it up as if making cabbage salad.

Add cabbage to saucepan along with the following ingredients:

    1 c. water
    1 tsp. salt
    1 tsp. sugar
    1 tsp. vinegar
    1 whole apple, diced (cored & peeled)
    1 bay leaf
    2 whole cloves
    1 pinch of flour, sprinkled over the top.

Cover and bring to boiling, reduce heat and cook until the apple pretty well dissolves. Check occasionally and stir. Add water as needed to avoid burning.

Spaghetti Sauce (Mrs. Irene Padgett)

Brown 1 lb of hamburger & drain (may use turkey burger)
1 tsp. salt
1 tsp. sugar
2 to 3 tsp. garlic powder
2 to 3 tsp. paprika
Dash of Thyme
2 to 3 tsp. chili powder
1 tsp. basil
1 bay leaf
½ lb sliced mushrooms
1 onion, diced
1 green pepper, diced
3 cans (6 oz) tomato paste
1 can (8 oz) tomato sauce
3 cans (8 oz) water

Mix all ingredients and let simmer at least 20 minutes.

APPENDIX

MEASURING

3 tsp. = 1 Tbsp	1 c. = 8 fluid oz
4 Tbsp. = ¼ c.	2 c. = 1 pint
5 1/3 Tbsp. = 1/3 c.	2 pint = 1 quart
16 Tbsp. = 1 c.	4 qt = 1 gallon

SUBSTITUTIONS & EQUIVALENTS

Cake Flour	1 c. minus 2 Tbsp. all purpose flour, well sifted, can substitute for 1 c. cake flour
Cornstarch (for thickening)	2 Tbsp. flour or 4 tsp. quick tapioca can substitute for 1 Tbsp. cornstarch
Baking Powder	¼ tsp. baking soda + ½ c. buttermilk can substitute for 1 tsp. baking powder (and ½ c. of liquid in the recipe)
Whole Milk	½ c. evaporated milk + ½ c. water, or 1 c. reconstituted dry milk + 2 ½ tsp. butter can substitute for 1 c. whole milk
Compressed Yeast cake	1 package or 2 tsp. active dry yeast can substitute for 1 cake of compressed yeast
Sour milk or buttermilk	1 Tbsp. lemon juice or vinegar + enough sweet milk to make 1 c. (let stand 5 minutes) can substitute for 1 c. sour milk/buttermilk
1 whole egg	2 egg yolks can substitute for 1 whole egg in custard recipes
Dry herbs	1 tsp. dried herbs = 1 Tbsp. fresh herbs
1 square (1 oz) unsweetened chocolate	3 Tbsp. cocoa + 1 Tbsp. butter can substitute for 1 square of unsweetened chocolate
Juice of 1 lemon	Equals about 3 Tbsp
Juice of 1 orange	Equals about 1/3 c.
Grated peel of 1 orange	Equals about 2 tsp
Grated peel of 1 lemon	Equals about 1 tsp